W9-BTL-191

POLAND

TEXT
Roman Marcinek

TRANSLATED BY
Krzysztof Kwaśniewicz

PHOTOGRAPHS
Ryszard Czerwiński, Michał Grychowski

KLUSZCZYŃSKI

ENGLISH LANGUAGE EDITOR
Jasper Tilbury

PHOTOGRAPHS

R. Czerwiński:

8/1, 12/1, 13/1, 14/1, 15/3, 16/1, 17/1, 18/1, 22/1, 25/2, 26/1, 17/2, 28, 30, 32, 33/2, 34/2, 34/3, 36, 39/2, 39/3, 40/1, 41/2, 41/3, 43, 44, 46/3,
50, 52, 53, 54, 55/1, 56, 58/2, 58/2, 58/3, 59, 62, 63, 66, 67/1, 68/1, 68/2, 69/3, 70/1, 71, 72, 73, 74, 76/1, 77, 78/2, 79/1, 80/1, 80/2, 81/1,
82/1, 83/2, 84/1, 84/2, 85/3, 87/1, 88, 89/2, 90, 91/2, 94/1, 94/3, 95/1, 96/1, 97/2, 98/2. 99/2, 99/1, 102, 103, 104, 105, 106, 107, 108/2, 109/1,
110, 111, 112, 113, 114/2, 115, 116/1, 116/3, 117, 118/1, 119/2, 120, 121/1, 122/1, 123/1, 124/1, 125/1, 126/2, 128/3

M. Grychowski:

7, 8/2, 9/2, 10, 11, 13/1, 14/2, 14/3, 15/1, 16/2, 16/3, 17/2, 17/3, 18/2, 19, 23/3, 24, 25/1, 26/2, 29/1, 31/1, 37, 38, 39/1, 40/2, 42, 45,
46/2, 46/2, 46/4, 47/2, 48, 49, 57, 58/1, 60, 61, 64, 65/1, 67/2, 68/3, 69/2, 78/1, 79/2, 80/3, 81/2, 82/2, 83/1, 84/3, 85/1, 85/2, 86/2, 87/2, 89/1,
91/1, 92, 93/2, 93/3, 94/2, 96/2, 97/1, 98/1, 99/2, 101, 123/2, 125/2, 125/3, 126/1, 127, 128/1, 128/2

Publisher's archives: 12/2, 34/1, 114/1, 119/1, 121/2, 121/3; J. Kozina: 9/1, 15/2, 20, 21, 22/2, 23/1, 23/2, 35, 100;
S. Markowski: 27/1, 41/1; BE&W Agency: 29/2, 47/1, 76/2, 95/2, 109/2, 116/2; PAP: 31/1, 65/2, 65/3; P. Komorowski; 70/2; E. Witecki: 75;
J. Nowakowski: 86/1; P. Tomczyk: 93/1; Ch. Parma: 108/1; Ch. Niedenthal: 118/2; ST Studio: 51/2, 55/2, 55/3;
St. Jabłońska: 122/2; H. Szymański: 124/2

MAP
Anna Gałuszka

DTP
look STUDIO, Kraków, ul. Wielopole 17,
tel./fax +48 (12) 429 18 31, e-mail look@kki.pl

ISBN: 83-88080-42-3

CONTENTS

Łeba

Gdańsk

Frombork

Lidzbark Warmiński

Bytów

MALBORK

Świeta Lipka

Trzęsacz

Pelplin

Kwidzyn

Kanał Augustowski

Kamień Pomorski

Tykocin

Białystok

Szczecin

Golub-Dobrzyń

Stargard Szczeciński

TORUŃ

Biskupin

Kruszwica

PUSZCZA BIAŁOWIESKA

Mogilno

Strzelno

Płock

Gniezno

Trzemeszno

Poznań

Kórnik

Ląd

Żelazowa Wola

WARSZAWA

Rogalin

Tum

Nieborów i Arkadia

Łódź

Puławy

Kazimierz Dolny

Lublin

Wrocław

Wąchock

Święty Krzyż

Opatów

ZAMOŚĆ

Krzeszów

Ksiąz

Brzeg

Częstochowa

Kielce

Ujazd

Wambierzyce

Opole

Ogrodzieniec

Sandomierz

Jędrzejów

Baranów

Pieskowa Skała

Wiślica

Leżajsk

Łańcut

KRAKÓW

Tarnów

Krasiczyn

Wadowice

WIELICZKA

Biecz

Ulucz

OŚWIĘCIM

Szalowa

KALWARIA ZEBRZYDOWSKA

Kwiatoń

Dębno

Niedzica

Zakopane

⬤ Sites on UNESCO's World Heritage List

● Other sites described in the book

INTRODUCTION

History is best appreciated at the places where it was made – palace chambers, cathedral naves, castle courtyards, merchant houses, university colleges, monastery cloisters. Historic locations are where politicians, artists, scholars, rulers and their subjects lived and worked. These places changed over time, reflecting current fashions and the changing fortunes of the nation. Today, we protect and cherish our historic inheritance, because whenever a monument of the past is lost, or a piece of landscape is destroyed, part of our national tradition dies. Or, perhaps, we should rather say "civic spirit", for throughout its history, Poland's power and prestige was built by people of various nationalities, religions and customs. They have left an extremely rich legacy – cathedrals, eastern-rite churches, synagogues, mosques; Gothic castles and granaries; wooden mills and stone penitential crosses; the Romanesque, Renaissance, Baroque, Art Nouveau…

The sites presented in this book are merely a sample of things worth seeing. Some readers may object that too little has been included. This is inevitable. Hard choices are necessary when there is so much to choose from.

From Opołonek, the southernmost peak in the Polish Bieszczady Mountains to Cape Rozewie at the very north, from Cedynia on the Odra to a bend in the Bug river on the eastern flank of the country, Poland abounds in natural wonders and historic sites. They may not be evenly distributed, but *every* region has something special to offer. One should also do justice to the great diversity of the landscape: from Alpine mountains to low-lying polders, from the largest marshland in Europe to a genuine sandy desert.

Poland lies at the heart of Europe, occupying the eastern part of the Central European Plain. The land inclines downwards from the southeast to the northwest. Thus, the highest point in Poland is Mount Rysy in the Tatra Mountains (2499 m above sea level), and the lowest lies in the Vistula Fens near Raczki Elbląskie (a depression of 1.8 metres).

Along the Baltic coast, the land is generally low-lying, especially in the valleys of the Vistula and Odra. The coastline is fairly straight, interrupted by just two major bays – the Bay of Pomerania and the Bay of Gdańsk. Even so, the coastal landscape is diversified with lagoons, lakes, dunes and sandy beaches. Steep cliffs are more the exception than the rule.

The coastal areas are adjoined on the south by lakelands, divided by the Vistula into two broad regions: the Pomeranian Lakeland to the west and the Masurian Lakeland to the east. The latter has a greater number of lakes, which, moreover, are bigger (hence its popular name: "The Great-Lake Country"). Further to the south is a lowland belt, comprising the Southern Wielkopolska Lowlands, Lower Silesian Plains and Mazovian Lowlands. Next there begins an upland belt with the Świętokrzyskie Mountains, the Cracow-Częstochowa Uplands and the Silesian Plateau. Poland's southern border is for the most part hilly, with the Sudetes to the west (the highest point – Mount Śnieżka; 1602 m above sea level) and the Carpathians to the east, comprising (apart from the Tatras), the Beskidy, Gorce, Pieniny and Bieszczady ranges.

There are about 9,300 lakes in Poland with an area exceeding one hectare. Most of these are situated in the northern lakeland areas. However, the Tatran lakes almost match the Masurian ones in depth. Poland's deepest lakes are Hańcza, Drawsko and Wigry in the Masurian Lakeland (108.5, 79.7 and 73.0 metres, respectively), while the two deepest Tatran lakes – Wielki Staw and Czarny Staw – measure, respectively, 79.3 and 76.4 metres. Nearly all of Poland (97%) is situated in the Baltic basin. Only small fragments of the Bieszczady and Beskidy mountains lie in the Black Sea basin, whereas the southern slopes of the Stołowe Mountains and Bystrzyckie Mountains belong to the North Sea basin.

Poland was among the first countries to adopt environmental protection measures. The chamois and the marmot have been protected in the Tatras since 1868 – longer than anywhere else in the world. Currently, there are more than 20 national parks in Poland, more than 100 areas of outstanding natural beauty, 250 protected landscape areas and more than 1,000 nature reserves. The function of national parks is to protect valuable biotopes that have been preserved in a more or less intact form. No commerce or industry is allowed in national parks, and the only form of human interference concerns the restoration of the environment and providing access for tourists.

Areas of outstanding natural beauty and protected landscape areas enjoy special treatment in view of their natural, historical or cultural specificity. They often cover extensive tracts of land. For instance, the Jurassic Protected Landscape Area (the oldest such area in Poland) extends along the Jurassic Uplands all the way from Cracow to Częstochowa, more than 100 km to the northwest. Nature reserves are the most numerous, and typically, the smallest protected areas. A strict reserve precludes all forms of human activity on its territory. Other reserves have been established in order to protect particular plant or animal species, or a specific type of environment.

Complementary to the natural surroundings is the historical environment. Poland is a successor to one of the most interesting political organisms that evolved in Europe during the last six centuries – the Polish-Lithuanian state, also known as the Commonwealth of the Two Nations. Cracow, and later Warsaw, were places where the fate of Central and Eastern Europe was decided – these were the capitals of a state that had to be reckoned with by emperors, czars, kings, sultans and khans; a kingdom whose throne was coveted by royalty from all over Europe.

The earliest remnants of settlement in Poland are approximately 500,000 years old. Slavonic tribes inhabited the area from the 5th or 6th century of the Christian era. In the 9th century, the Polanians attained a dominant position, and in 966 their ruler Mieszko embraced Christianity. During the reign of his son and successor, Bolesław the Brave, the first Polish bishoprics were established, and Bolesław himself was crowned as the first king of Poland (1025). Following a period of disintegration after his death, the Polish state was rebuilt and strengthened by Kazimierz the Restorer and Bolesław the Bold. Bolesław the Wry-mouthed subdued Pomerania for a short while, but his testament of 1138 provided for the division of the country between his sons. Nearly 200 years of fragmentation ensued, and it was not until 1320 that Poland finally became reunited under a new king, Władysław the Elbow-High. During the reign of his son, Kazimierz the Great, the state underwent consolidation, although it was too weak to claim the remainder of its provinces. Increased contacts with the east led to the Polish-Lithuanian Union of Krewo in 1385 and the beginning of a new dynasty – the Jagiellons, under whom Poland reached the apogee of its power. Its archenemy, the Teutonic Order, was defeated, the Tartar invasions, which had wreaked havoc in the country on several occasions, were curbed, and a period of unprecedented economic and cultural development followed. Unfortunately, this was also the time when the balance of power was ultimately and irrevocably tipped in favour of the nobility. Progressing anarchy and a series of wars in the 17th century left Poland greatly weakened (despite some spectacular military victories). The 18th century saw Poland gradually lose its independence, which neither the belated reforms (including the Constitution of 3 May 1791), nor the patriotic and cultural revival of the final quarter of the century, could avert. The three partitions of Poland (in 1772, 1793 and 1795, respectively), effected by her neighbours – Russia, Prussia and Austria – obliterated the Polish state from the map of Europe.

It was hoped that Poland would regain independence thanks to Napoleon, but his defeat put an end to those dreams. At the Congress of Vienna in 1815, the final borders between the partitioning powers were drawn: Russia was to occupy the eastern part of Poland (including Warsaw), Prussia – Wielkopolska and Pomerania, and Austria – the southern part of the country, roughly corresponding to Małopolska (referred to by the Austrians as the provinces of "Galicia and Lodomeria"). The two insurrections (of 1830–1831 and 1863–1864) staged in the "Kingdom of Poland" – as the Russian partition was then officially called – were as heroic as they were futile. The "Kingdom of Poland" was directly incorporated into Russia and massive repression combined with intense Russification followed. Likewise, from 1871, Wielkopolska became subject to a ruthless campaign of Germanisation. By contrast, Galicia was allowed to form a local parliament in 1861, and from 1867 was gradually shifting towards autonomy, with beneficial results in the spheres of culture and science.

The First World War revived Polish hopes for a change of fortune. And indeed, the outcome of the war was favourable: with Germany and Austria defeated, and Russia engulfed in a revolution, on 11 November 1918 Poland declared independence. The borders of the new Republic were established in the course of the ensuing Polish-Bolshevik war (1919–1920) and Silesian Uprisings (1919––1921). Polish governments now faced the problem of how to re-integrate provinces which had evolved for nearly 150 years under very different systems. This task was rendered even more difficult by political instability and economic crisis. Even so, the integration efforts brought admirable results and Poland finally entered the path of economic development.

But all too soon this was cut short by the German invasion of 1 September 1939, followed by a Soviet attack 16 days later. Poland's Western allies failed to fulfil their guarantees, and after little more than a month of fighting, Poland was partitioned once again: this time between Nazi Germany and the Soviet Union (in accordance with an agreement concluded by these two states on 23 August 1939). The western part of Poland was partly incorporated into the Reich, with the rest forming the so-called General-Government under Nazi rule; the eastern part was annexed by Stalin. A time of persecution, terror, deportations and extermination – directed especially against the Jewish

population – had begun. But the Poles continued to fight, both on the home front (the Home Army and various other underground and partisan units) and on all the fronts of the Second World War, until the ultimate fall of the Third Reich

Yet the taste of victory was bitter. As a result of the agreements concluded by the Big Three (Great Britain, Soviet Union, USA) at Teheran (1943) and Yalta (1945), Poland found itself in the Soviet sphere of influence. An inefficient command economy, suppression of civil liberties, political persecution, and periodic riots put down by brute force – this is what the greater part of the post-war years was like. Occasional periods of liberalisation were short-lived and attempts at economic reform proved abortive.

Radical change came about only in 1989, when the Round Table talks between the government and Solidarity led to partly free parliamentary elections, which turned into a landslide for the opposition. As a result, the first non-Communist government of post-war Poland came into being. A comprehensive programme of economic and constitutional reform was launched. Poland has now joined NATO and is aspiring to full membership in the European Union.

Visiting historic locations makes one realise that history is more than facts, names and dates. On seeing the sites where history was made, one might reflect on the spirit of the time and place and on the meaning of the associated tradition. In Poland, this is mainly the tradition of freedom and tolerance, the tradition of a multi-ethnic state, a close-knit union of Poles and Lithuanians, where other nations – Ruthenians, Jews, Germans, as well as Tartars, Russians, Greeks, Armenians, Scots, Irish, French and others – also lived, making a unique and valuable contribution to the vast inheritance of the Commonwealth of the Two Nations.

Hospitality and openness to foreigners have remained a national characteristic of the Poles – a trait that should make a visit to Poland all the more enjoyable.

Roman Marcinek (b. 1962) *graduated in history from the Jagiellonian University in Cracow. He is currently Head of the Regional Centre for Cultural Environment Protection and Studies in Cracow, a branch of the National Centre for Cultural Heritage Documentation. Mr. Marcinek has authored and co-authored numerous papers, documentation materials and programmes related to historical inheritance preservation and landscape protection, and has published articles in the field of archive studies. He is editor of* Teki Krakowskie, *a quarterly devoted to the protection of the historical inheritance, and has done editorial work for various publishing houses. As a sideline, he writes books and articles on military history.*

* * *

N.B. The arrow signs in the page footers (➡) refer the reader to other places of interest, not included in the text. These may be situated at the location in question or in its environs – sometimes in a rather inclusive sense of the term.

M A Ł O P O L S K A

Few regions in Poland are as beautiful or as rich in historical landmarks as Małopolska. This name is applied these days to a small section of a once enormous province which rated among the most important historical regions in Central Europe. Few people remember today that the huge Cracow diocese abutted on the Lithuanian borderland. The name Małopolska came into use only in the late 15th century; previously the region had been known as the Duchy of Cracow and Sandomierz. The ducal throne in Cracow was the object of bitter struggle among the princes of the Piast dynasty in the 12th-14th centuries, as a result of which it was local magnates who largely assumed control of the state in subsequent centuries. Once the capital of Poland had moved to Cracow in 1038, the town began to flourish. The patronage of the King and magnates, the wealth of the merchants and craftsmen, the power of the bishops and the prestige of the Cracow Academy – all these factors contributed to Cracow's position as a leading European centre of learning, art and commerce. Małopolska was the most important land of the Polish Crown. In the 15th century, it absorbed the neighbouring duchies of Oświęcim, Zator and Siewierz, and in the following century, also the Ukrainian lands under Polish rule. During the Partitions of Poland in the late 18th century, Małopolska was occupied by the Austrians and became severed from other parts of country until the early 20th century.

Małopolska abounds in monuments to its glorious past, framed in picturesque scenery. In the Małopolska Uplands, the ruins of medieval castles perched on limestone rocks merge into the beautiful Jurassic landscape. The most valuable parts of the natural and cultural heritage of this area have been incorporated in the Ojców National Park. Other areas of outstanding natural beauty, further away from Cracow, include the ancient Świętokrzyskie Mountains with the Puszcza Jodłowa forest and the Roztocze uplands with the Puszcza Solska forest. And everywhere, nature is interspersed with remnants of the country's splendid past, such as the towns of Sandomierz, Kazimierz on the Vistula, Lublin and Zamość.

1. Wawel Castle.
2. The "Zygmunt" Bell in Wawel Cathedral.

CRACOW – WAWEL CATHEDRAL

If one were to name the single most important place in the Polish national tradition, it would undoubtedly have to be Wawel Castle, a site of unsurpassed historical and artistic rank, built atop a hill overlooking the Vistula, side by side with the Cathedral – a proud symbol of Poland's religious heritage. Culturally, Wawel Hill outranks the entire city of Cracow, having attained the status of a national Pantheon.

The construction of the Cathedral – now under the triple patronage of SS Wacław, Stanisław and the Holy Saviour – was commenced upon the establishment of the Cracow diocese in the year 1000. Only small vestiges have survived of the Romanesque church built by King Bolesław the Brave, supplanted with the aisled basilica erected during the reign of King Władysław Herman (1079-1102) and completed in 1142. Parts of that latter structure are still to be seen: St. Leonard's Crypt – a Romanesque chamber with a vault supported on two rows of pillars – and remnants of two towers, including a section of stone wall in the Cathedral's southern tower, known as the Silver Bell Tower. King Władysław's Cathedral burnt down in 1305.

The next, Gothic church was built on the site in the years 1320-1364. It was completed during the reign of King Kazimierz the Great, whose monogram adorns the magnificent wrought-iron door at the main west entrance.

Today, the Cathedral is a brick-and-stone basilica with a transept and ambulatory lined with chapels, two of which are especially noteworthy: the Renaissance Zygmunt Chapel and the adjacent Vasa Chapel (1664-1666). One of the three Cathedral towers boasts the 11-ton "Zygmunt" Bell (the work of Hans Beham from 1520), whose dignified toll can now only be heard on major church and state holidays. The first Polish King to be crowned there (in the burnt-out shell of Władysław Herman's Cathedral) was Władysław the Elbow-High, who was also the first ruler of Poland to be buried in the Cathedral. Many other kings and national heroes have their tombs in the aisles and crypt. To the south and west, the Cathedral is surrounded by a wall with gates, built in 1619.

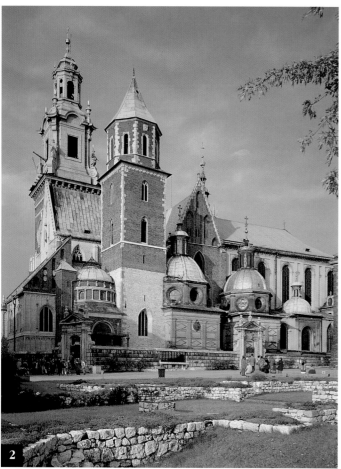

1. St. Leonard's Crypt.
2. Wawel Cathedral.

➡ Some of the best views of the city are to be had from its four "Mounds", dedicated to legendary and modern heroes: Krakus (7th cent.), Wanda (8th cent.), Kościuszko (19th cent.) and Piłsudski (20th cent.).

The Cathedral interior is a veritable treasure-trove, full of relics of the past. The central part of the nave is occupied by a Baroque shrine holding the remains of St. Stanisław – the martyr patron-saint of Cracow – designed by Giovanni Trevano. It was constructed in 1626-1629, at the spot where the remains of St. Florian and St. Stanisław had been interred in 1184 and 1254, respectively. It is a sacred place, where Polish rulers would offer their war trophies, including the Teutonic Knights' standards captured at the battle of Grunwald in 1410.

The royal tombs in the Cathedral immediately catch the eye, in particular the Gothic sarcophagi of Władysław the Elbow-High, who reunited the Polish state in the 14th century after a period of disintegration, Kazimierz the Great, who prepared the ground for Poland's tremendous development in subsequent centuries, and Władysław Jagiełło, the architect of the Polish-Lithuanian Union. Artistically, the most impressive is Kazimierz the Jagiellon's sarcophagus, made by Veit Stoss in 1492. The Renaissance-style tombs of the last Jagiellons and the Mannerist monument to Stephen Bathory from 1595 are not to be missed either. The "Black Crucifix" in the ambulatory, which is an object of great veneration, dates back to the 14th century.

Housed in the Cathedral Treasury and in the nearby Cathedral Museum are monuments from all epochs of the past, rare objects of religious art and other items of historical interest. The highlights of the collection include a reliquary holding the head of St. Stanisław, a liturgical cross made of royal diadems, and the spear of St. Maurice, donated to Bolesław the Brave by Emperor Otto III on the occasion of the latter's visit to Gniezno in AD 1000, as a token of recognition of the Polish Prince's sovereignty. While in the Cathedral, one should also see the Holy Cross Chapel, adorned with Byzantine-Ruthenian-style murals, and descend to the crypt to see the tombs of Polish kings and national heroes (including Marshal Józef Piłsudski and the poets Adam Mickiewicz and Juliusz Słowacki). The long and steep ascent to the top of the Zygmunt Tower is rewarded by a breathtaking view over Cracow's Old Town.

1

2

1. *Piotr Kmita's chasuble.*
2. *St. Stanisław' coffin in Wawel Cathedral.*

➡ The 17th-century Bernardine monastery and church, with its imposing high altar and mausoleum of the Blessed Szymon of Lipnica.

1. Altar in the Zygmunt Chapel (1531-1538).
2. Eagle motif from the monument of King Zygmunt August.
3. Tombs of the last Jagiellons.

➡ The Pauline "Skałka" Church designed in Roman Baroque style, the burial place of many famous Poles; the Rakowicki Cemetery – one of the oldest and largest Polish necropolises.

CRACOW – WAWEL CATHEDRAL

In the 16th century, a magnificent mausoleum of the last kings of the Jagellonian dynasty was appended to the Cathedral. The Zygmunt Chapel, which has been preserved to this day in its original shape, is considered to be the high point of Renaissance architecture in Central Europe. It was erected in 1519-1530 (replacing a former chapel founded ca. 1340 by Kazimierz the Great) by Bartolomeo Berrecci from Tuscany, aided by the best Italian architects working in Poland at the time. Berrecci – an architect and sculptor – had come to Cracow ca. 1516 to enter the service of King Zygmunt I. In 1537, he was stabbed to death by a jealous compatriot.

The direct cause of the foundation of the Chapel was the death of the King's first wife, Barbara Zapolya. The Chapel was built on a square plan, its main body topped by an octagonal drum supporting the distinctive dome, which was gilded in 1591-1592 by order of Queen Anna the Jagiellon.

The interior decoration of sandstone and red marble incorporates mythological, secular and religious scenes, animal and floral motifs, and Christian and pagan themes. The tomb of King Zygmunt August and the figure of Queen Anna were sculpted by Santi Gucci, but the authorship of Zygmunt I's monument is still disputed (probably it was the work of Berrecci, though some historians attribute it to Giovanni Padovano). The fine altarpiece (1531-1538) made by Nuremberg masters was donated by Zygmunt I. Its central panel and part of the wings show scenes from the life of the Blessed Virgin Mary, wrought in silver. The chapel is separated from the Cathedral ambulatory by an elaborate grille dating from the first half of the 16th century, whose lower part is the work of Nuremberg artists.

Opposite the chapel entrance, the noble simplicity of Queen Jadwiga's sarcophagus, put up in 1902 by order of Karol Lanckoroński, immediately catches the eye. The sculptor Antoni Madeyski enshrined in white Carrara marble the legend of the beautiful and kind-hearted Lady of Wawel Castle. The actual tomb of the Queen, who died in 1399, is situated in front of the high altar.

1. Wawel Cathedral interior.
2. Liturgical cross fashioned from ducal diadems; 13th cent.
3. Spear of St. Maurice.

➡ The fortified Premonstratensian monastery and church in Cracow's Zwierzyniec district; the nearby Church of the Saviour is one of the oldest in Poland.

CRACOW – WAWEL CASTLE

A fortified settlement on top of Wawel Hill was already the centre of the Vistulanian state in the 8th century. The surviving remnants of stonework and the pre-Romanesque rotunda of SS Felix and Adauctus date back to the early Piast period of the 10th century. The first Polish ruler of that dynasty to choose Wawel as his permanent residence was Prince Kazimierz the Restorer (1040-1058). The Royal Castle, which now houses the State Art Collections, has undergone innumerable changes since.

The earliest part of the Gothic castle was a tower built of unhewn limestone. In the 19th century, it was dubbed "Łokietek Tower", but in reality it was probably erected by Vaclav II from the Bohemian Premyslid dynasty. Subsequently, a perimeter wall was raised to protect the buildings scattered about the irregularly-shaped courtyard. In the mid-14th century, Kazimierz the Great had a sizeable castle built on Wawel Hill (subsequently enlarged). Two other towers – the Jordanka and the Thieves' Tower – are also usually dated to the times of King Kazimierz. The surviving fragments of the Gothic castle include two other towers, known as the "Danish Tower" and the "Hen's Foot" (15th century). Two more towers were raised during Kazimierz the Jagiellon's reign: the Senators' Tower (formerly called "Lubranka") and the Sandomierz Tower.

The royal seat at Wawel flourished during the reign of Zygmunt the Old, who decided to transform the Gothic castle into a Renaissance-style residence fit for a ruler of one of the greatest European powers. Remodelling work had already commenced under the guidance of the architect and sculptor Francesco Fiorentino, who in 1502-1507 rebuilt the castle's western wing as the so-called "Queen's House". When Zygmunt acceded to the throne, he continued his plans (from 1507 until 1536), with the assistance of Fiorentino (until 1516), Master Benedict (1521?-1529) and, most important of all, Bartolomeo Berrecci (1530-1536). Thus, on Wawel Hill there arose a splendid palace with an arcaded courtyard – a source of enjoyment and pride for generations to come.

1. Wawel Castle courtyard.
2. Szczerbiec, or the "Notched Sword", the coronation sword of Polish kings.

➡ The Church of St. Catherine with the former Augustinian monastery – one of the largest and most beautiful Gothic basilicas in Poland.

The interiors of Wawel are a fitting complement to the castle's monumental architecture. Artists commissioned by the Jagiellons decorated them with paintings, friezes, coffered ceilings and richly adorned portals. The most magnificent room of all is the Audience Hall, also known as the Envoys' Chamber, which has remarkable coffered ceiling decorated with wooden, polychrome heads looking down from the caissons. These realistic sculptures, dating from the years 1531-1535, represent a collective portrait of Cracow society of the time. They inspired many legends, the best known of which recalls the story of a head which admonished King Zygmunt August for passing an unjust judgement. The King then ordered an artist to gag the defiant head.

Zygmunt August enriched the decoration of the Wawel chambers with an enormous set of Flemish tapestries. He had been collecting them since ca. 1553, and in 1571 bequeathed them to the Polish State. Many of the surviving 142 tapestries make up cycles, such as *Paradise*, *Story of Noah* or *Construction of the Tower of Babel*. Others show imaginary landscapes, animal scenes, heraldic elements, royal monograms and grotesque motifs.

The Treasury and Armoury, accessible from the courtyard, are also a must for the visitor. One of the exhibits is *Szczerbiec* – the "notched sword" used at the coronation ceremonies of Polish kings. Legend has it the weapon belonged to Bolesław the Brave, the first ruler to be crowned King of Poland.

The fire of 1595, which ruined the castle, was one of the reasons the royal court moved to Warsaw. King Zygmunt III Vasa had part of the palace rebuilt, with elements of early Baroque style, but the royal residence was dealt a decisive blow during the Swedish invasions of 1655 and 1702, when it was plundered and twice burnt to the ground. After the Partitions of Poland, Wawel Castle fell into ruin. In 1846, the Austrians converted it into barracks. They tore down the medieval walls and towers encircling the hill and replaced them with heavy brick bastions that made Wawel look like a citadel pointing its guns at Cracow. The repurchase of the castle from the army in 1905 was an event of nationwide importance. Subsequent painstaking restoration work was funded by lavish public donations.

1. The "Wawel Heads" – ceiling decoration.
2. Envoys' Chamber.

➡ The Church of SS Peter and Paul – the first Baroque-style church in Poland, erected by Giovanni Trevano, the burial place of the famous preacher Piotr Skarga.

CRACOW

At the foot of Wawel Hill lies the ancient town of Cracow, one of the chief attractions of this part of Europe. Having descended the hill, you can walk towards the centre along Kanonicza Street, passing on your way the outstanding houses and palaces that used to belong to the canons of the Cracow Chapter.

The earliest recorded mention of Cracow dates from 965; in 1038, the town became Poland's capital and the seat of its monarchs – a position it held until the end of the 16th century. The settlements which clustered around Wawel Hill evolved in time into a fully-fledged town. At the turn of the 11th century, the first imposing buildings in Romanesque style were raised (St. Andrew's Church, for instance, now with a Baroque interior). New settlements clung to the route leading from the town northwards, with churches (for example, St. Mary's, 1226) and monasteries (Dominican, 1222; Franciscan, 1237) of their own. The growth of the town was checked by the Tartar invasion of 1241. In 1257, Prince Bolesław the Chaste granted Cracow a municipal charter, allotting the task of planning and building a new town to Silesian settlers. It was at that time that Cracow received its regular, geometrical layout, with a large market square situated at the centre of a grid of streets.

The 14th and early 15th centuries were a time of rapid development for Cracow. It was then that the most important municipal buildings were constructed, concentrated in and around the market square – the Town Hall, the Cloth Hall and numerous churches in the local variant of Gothic style. The Renaissance likewise left its imprint on the appearance of the town. It can be seen, for instance, in the omnipresent parapet, so characteristic of Polish architecture of the period. When King Zygmunt III Vasa moved the capital to Warsaw at the turn of the 16th century, the town's potential for expansion subsided, and Cracow turned gradually from a bustling European metropolis into an atmospheric old town. Today, it is a major centre of industry, tourism and learning.

1. The Romanesque Church of St. Andrew.
2. Interior of St. Andrew's: a Baroque pulpit.
3. Kanonicza Street.

➡ Cricot 2 Theatre Archive, where the spirit of the great avant-garde playwright Tadeusz Kantor lives on.

Together with a municipal charter, Cracow received its regular layout based on a rectangular grid centred on a 200 × 200 m market square. The latter has never ceased to impress visitors with its dimensions and beautiful architecture. Medieval buildings in the main market square include the diminutive St. Adalbert's Church (which supposedly marks the place where the martyr would preach), fragments of which date from before the Tartar invasion of 1241, the Town Hall tower (before 1383), St. Mary's Church, numerous houses, and the unmistakable Cloth Hall.

The Cloth Hall is the most famous medieval trading establishment and one of the best known historical monuments in Poland. It was built in 1380-1400 under the supervision of M. Lindintolde, incorporating the stalls where imported cloth had been traded since the late 13th century. In 1555, the Cloth Hall burnt down, and the municipal authorities entrusted the task of reconstructing it to Giovanni Padovano. The building was given a Renaissance appearance with tunnel vaults and lunettes, above which an upper floor was crowned with a parapet featuring a row of mascarons (attributed to Santi Gucci), a truly remarkable collection of Renaissance decorative sculpture. Additional entrances were made in 1601, so that the communication lines within the building now took the shape of a cross.

The building fell into disrepair in the 18th-19th centuries, together with the entire town. It was only rarely used for formal ceremonies (for example, on the occasion of the visit of King Stanisław August Poniatowski in 1787, or a ball held in honour of Prince Józef Poniatowski in 1809). Restoration of the Cloth Hall began in 1875. Upon the recommendation of the famous painter Jan Matejko, supervision of the work was entrusted to promising young architect Tomasz Pryliński. The upper floor was converted into reception rooms, which have been in the possession of the National Museum since 1900. Today, they house a Gallery of Polish Painting from the 18th and 19th centuries. The ground floor remains Cracow's most attractive shopping arcade. Together with the pigeons, flower-sellers, the rather unsightly, but dearly loved monument to Adam Mickiewicz, and countless little restaurants and cafés – the Cloth Hall contributes to the unique atmosphere of Cracow's Main Market Square.

1. St. Adalbert's Church from pre-charter times.
2. The Cloth Hall Gallery: Foursome by Józef Chełmoński.
3. The Cloth Hall and monument to Mickiewicz.

➡ Old Town streets and corners; the "Small" Market Square.

CRACOW

The Cloth Hall was meant to be a sign of Cracow's prosperity. By the same token, St. Mary's Church was to bear witness to the piety of the city's inhabitants. It is an aisled Gothic basilica with a transept, erected in the early 14th century in place of an old Romanesque church destroyed by the Tartars in 1241. The new brick church was completed before 1320. Construction of the chancel in the years 1355-1365 was commissioned by Mikołaj Wierzynek the Elder of Sandomierz. The original hall design was converted into a basilica by Mikołaj Werner in 1392-1397, and the surrounding chapels were added in 1435-1446. Further alterations followed, including Baroque interior decoration by Francesco Placidi and the construction of an impressive porch at the main entrance in the 18th century.

Two towers rise above the façade of the Church on the Market Square side, the taller of which (80 m) is called the Bugle Tower. Every hour a bugle call is sounded from the tower by a fireman. This custom has been cultivated, albeit irregularly, since the Middle Ages. It is thought to commemorate a watchman who raised the alarm upon seeing the approaching Tartars and was killed by an arrow. This is why the call ends unexpectedly in the middle of a bar. The lower tower houses five bells, the largest of which (known as the "Half-Zygmunt") was allegedly carried to the top of the tower single-handedly in 1438 by one Stanisław Ciołek, noted for his superhuman strength. Another bell, "Tenebrat", was sounded only during executions of criminals. The nave is lit by medieval stained-glass windows from 1370-1400 (now restored, as is the entire church interior). These harmonise well with the stained-glass designs by the Art Nouveau artists Józef Mehoffer and Stanisław Wyspiański. The chancel has polychrome decoration executed by Jan Matejko in 1889-1892. Many furnishings have been preserved in the church, including a stone crucifix by Veit Stoss, early-Baroque stalls, epitaphs of wealthy Cracow burghers and charming side chapels. The church treasury contains an impressive collection of liturgical vessels and vestments.

1. St. Mary's Church.
2. Nave of St. Mary's with Veit Stoss's altar.
3. Gothic chalice with the Łabędź ("Swan") coat-of-arms, St. Mary's Treasury.

➤ Franciscan Church and Monastery (13th cent.), with Art Nouveau stained-glass windows and a portrait gallery of Cracow bishops in the cloisters.

The highlight of the interior is the stunning high altar – a polyptych made of oak and linden wood, measuring 11 × 13 m, one of the greatest achievements of European art of the late Middle Ages. It was carved in 1477-1489 by a Nuremberg citizen of Swabian origin, Veit Stoss (ca. 1445––1533).

Stoss lived in Poland until 1496, working mainly for rich Cracow burghers and influential officials from the royal court. Stoss is considered one of the greatest German artists of the late Gothic period. While in Cracow, he mainly designed sepulchral monuments and religious sculpture. He switched easily between dramatic forms full of pathos, and a stylised approach marked by humanistic simplicity and decorative appearance. His remuneration for the work was 2808 florins – an amount equivalent to the town's annual budget!

This is one of the largest existing winged altars. It consists of a retable with three-dimensional figures, and two pairs of wings covered with reliefs.

The altar can be opened to reveal a scene of the Dormition and Assumption of the Blessed Virgin Mary and events connected with the Birth and Resurrection of Christ. The outer panels on one pair of wings show Passion scenes, while the open-work crowning of the retable contains a Coronation-of-Our-Lady group and figures of SS Stanisław and Adalbert, the patron saints of Poland. The subject matter of the predella is the Jesse Tree, or the genealogy of Jesus and Mary.

The figures sculpted by Stoss exhibit highly individualised features and dramatic facial expressions, emphasised by the dynamic postures. Their robes fold richly in elaborate, decorative patterns characteristic of Stoss's art. The artist carved the entire enormous altarpiece almost single-handedly – only a few details of secondary importance were executed by his students.

During the Second World War, the altarpiece was seized by the Germans and transported to the Reich, ending up in Nuremberg. After restoration, it was first exhibited at Wawel Castle, and in 1957 it returned to where it belongs – in the chancel of St. Mary's Church.

1. Detail from Veit Stoss's altar.
2. Crucifixion, a 14th century stained-glass window in St. Mary's Church.
3. Monuments to the Montelupi family in St. Mary's Church.

➡ Dominican Church and Monastery (14th cent.), with the St. Hyacinth chapel and a cloister lined with epitaphs; the chancel is the burial place of Prince Leszek the Black.

CRACOW

With its growing prosperity, Cracow needed to protect the life and property of its citizens. Towards the end of the 13th century, the construction of fortifications began (authorised by Prince Leszek the Black in 1285), which took their final shape in the 14th century, thanks to the efforts of Kings Vaclav II, Władysław the Elbow-High and Kazimierz the Great. Originally, the town was girded by a double ring of walls, the inner one additionally protected by several dozen towers. Regrettably, the walls were pulled down in the first half of the 19th century, save for a short section on either side of the St. Florian Gate (Brama Floriańska), including the Carpenters' (Ciesielska), Haberdashers' (Pasamoników) and Joiners' (Stolarska) Towers. The gate itself was spared, too – the only one of ten to survive. Like the walls and the remaining towers, it was built of stone in its lower part (dating from the turn of the 13th century), with a brick superstructure added in the 15th century. The towers were linked by a gallery running along the wall, now reconstructed. Another preserved part of the city fortifications is the City Arsenal, which today houses part of the Czartoryski Museum. Yet another structure which luckily escaped the destructive craze of the 19th century was the Cracow Barbican – a remarkable late Gothic monument of military architecture. This semi-circular outwork, with 3-metre thick walls and an inner courtyard (24.5 metres wide), was built in 1498-1499 during the reign of King Jan Olbracht, and offered additional security against the threat of an Ottoman siege. The Barbican was surrounded at that time with a 24-metre-wide moat with a sluice system, and its lower part was shielded with a rampart. Loopholes at three levels allowed the defenders tremendous firepower. The machicolated upper gallery was crowned with seven observation turrets. When Cracow came under siege in 1581, 1655 and 1768, the Barbican served its purpose extremely well. In times of peace, the adjacent St. Florian's Gate was the *Porta Gloriae*, or the "Gate of Glory", opening the Royal Way to Wawel Castle. Today, the Old Town is surrounded by a park which follows the line of the former walls. The preserved section of wall serves as a kind of outdoor gallery, which lends the place a special atmosphere.

1. The Barbican.
2. The Carpenters' Tower.

➡ The *Planty* – a green ring surrounding the Old Town, adorned by neat flowerbeds and dotted with numerous statues.

It was largely up to the inhabitants to defend their city in time of need. Each tower, gate or section of wall was assigned to a different guild, responsible for its maintenance in peace and defence in war. In order to keep up their combat readiness, people joined rifle guilds, whose principal aim was to train members in the use of firearms. Such guilds became widespread in Małopolska in the 14th century, although in Cracow their earliest credible mention dates from 1455. The rifle guilds would practise shooting at a range outside the town's perimeter, where they would also hold a prestigious annual contest. Members would shoot at a wooden decoy, and the contestant who shot off its last fragment would hold the guild's supreme office for the year to come. King Kazimierz the Jagiellon was a great enthusiast of shooting contests and offered expensive prizes to the winners. An ordinance issued by King Zygmunt August in 1562 exempted the best marksman of the rifle guilds from municipal taxes; King Władysław IV extended the scope of this privilege to include tolls and customs duties. The rifle guilds movement began to lose momentum from the 16th century onwards. Even so, a Cracow burgher named Marcin Oracewicz managed to shoot dead the commander of the Russian force besieging the city in 1768. Interestingly, he had loaded his rifle with a mantle button, for lack of ammunition. The sharpshooters' tradition is maintained today by local traders and craftsmen, with the top marksman being enthroned each year in a solemn ceremony.

Another delightful tradition is that of *Lajkonik*, originally developed by raftsmen from the Zwierzyniec district. It goes back to the Tartar invasions of the Middle Ages: *Lajkonik* is a bricklayer (originally, a raftsman) dressed up as a Tartar chieftain, who rides a richly adorned hobbyhorse from the Premonstratensian monastery at Zwierzyniec to the Main Market Square in the week following the Feast of Corpus Christi. Baton in hand, *Lajkonik* liberally swings blows at onlookers, which is supposed to bring them good luck. Legend has it that the event commemorates the Cracow raftsmen's victory over the Tartar invaders in the 13th century.

In the mid-19th century, the Austrians built a ring of fortifications around Cracow, which proved useful in the early days of the First World War. There were about 60 forts in all, several of which were pulled down in the 1950s, but even so the former Cracow fortress remains Poland's largest historical complex of military architecture.

1. Lajkonik.
2. The Silver Cockerel, the emblem of the Cracow rifle guild.
3. Cafés by the Cloth Hall.

➡ The Historical Museum of Cracow, featuring, among other things, interior decoration, locally-made nativity crèches, military equipment, clocks, as well as arts and crafts.

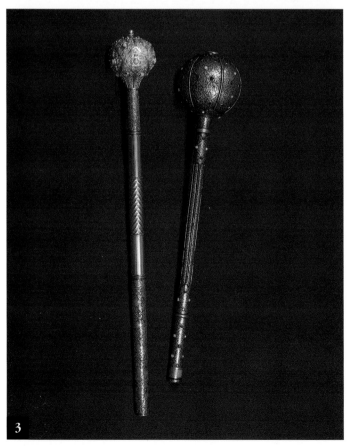

CRACOW

The Czartoryski Museum, situated by the city walls, is generally considered to be the oldest museum in Poland. It evolved from a collection of Polish and European memorabilia gathered by Princess Izabela Czartoryska at her family's estate in Puławy, southeastern Poland. The rank of her collection was enhanced by significant works of art by Leonardo da Vinci, Raphael and Rembrandt. During the November Uprising (1830-1831), the collection was saved from pillage, moving first to Sieniawa and then to Paris. In the 1870s, it was decided that the collection should return to Poland and be displayed in Cracow, where a museum was opened to this end in 1876. During the Second World War, the Museum was plundered by the Nazis, who took away the "Royal Casket" containing valuables that once belonged to Polish kings, and many other items, including old jewellery, a precious coin collection and, worst of all, the paintings by Leonardo da Vinci, Raphael and Rembrandt. The Leonardo and Rembrandt were recovered after the war, but Raphael's *Portrait of a Youth* disappeared forever without trace. The Museum also houses the priceless Czartoryski Library, which consists of both printed books and manuscripts.

The National Museum was founded by the City Council in 1879. From the very outset it made an important contribution to the cultural and artistic life of the city, for instance, by organising exhibitions on the bicentennial of the Battle of Vienna in 1883 and the tricentennial of the death of the poet Jan Kochanowski a year later. The collection grew and the Museum acquired buildings for its newly-created branches. Today, the Museum holds ca. 700 thousand items, some of exceptional cultural importance, and large series of paintings by Jan Matejko, Piotr Michałowski, Stanisław Wyspiański, Jacek Malczewski and many others. Apart from the main building – where the military and arts-and-crafts collections, as well as the 20th-Century Gallery of Polish Painting, are housed – the other branches of the National Museum include the Szołayski House, the Cloth Hall Gallery, Jan Matejko's House, and the Stanisław Wyspiański Museum.

1. Leonardo da Vinci, Lady with an Ermine; *Czartoryski Museum.*
2. Hussar's armour; *Czartoryski Museum.*
3. Commander-in-chief's batons; *Czartoryski Museum.*

➡ The Piarist Church of the Transfiguration, built in 1718-1759 by Kasper Bażanka and Francesco Placidi.

1. Stanisław Wyspiański, Maternity; *National Museum.*
2. *The Gothic Madonna of Krużlowa; National Museum.*
3. *Belts known as "Przeworsk-type" (18th cent.); National Museum.*

➡ The Aviation and Spaceflight Museum at Czyżyny – one of the best aircraft and engine collections in Europe.

CRACOW

The Jagellonian University, the oldest in Central Europe after the Charles University in Prague, was established twice. In 1364, it was founded (as the Cracow Academy) by King Kazimierz the Great, following the models of the legal faculties at Bologna and Padua. After Kazimierz's death, the Academy went into a decline. It was re-established by King Władysław Jagiełło in 1400, thanks to a bequest made by his deceased wife, Queen Jadwiga. This time it was patterned on the Theological University of Paris and had the four faculties usual for those times: law, medicine, theology, and the liberal arts. The Cracow Academy thrived in the 15th and first half of the 16th centuries. Its professors, Stanisław of Skarbimierz and Paweł Włodkowic were the first to formulate the idea of the rights of nations and a just war, as well as the principle of tolerance towards infidels. The Polish elites were educated at the Academy – among its students were, *inter alia*, Nicolaus Copernicus, the poets Jan Kochanowski and Szymon Szymonowic, the political thinker Andrzej Frycz-Modrzewski, the writer Mikołaj Rej, the theologian Stanisław Hozjusz, and the preacher Piotr Skarga. In the mid-16th century, standards declined once again and a long period of stagnation followed. Things changed for the better only with the establishment of the National Education Commission, which initiated reform of the University, carried out in 1780 by its graduate, Hugo Kołłątaj. After the annexation of Cracow by Austria, the University was Germanised, and many chairs were taken over by German scholars. Following Cracow's incorporation into the Duchy of Warsaw, the school was partly re-Polonised in 1809. The granting of autonomy by the Austrians to the province of Galicia in 1870 made possible the complete re-Polonisation of the University, which soon began to flourish. However, its rapid development was brutally interrupted by the outbreak of the Second World War and the treacherous arrest of 183 professors by the Nazis, who looted the libraries and vandalised the laboratories. Nowadays, the Jagellonian University is once again one of the largest academic institutions in Poland, involved in co-operation and exchange programmes with the world's major centres of learning.

1. Jagellonian University, the courtyard of Collegium Maius.
2. The "Jagellonian Globe" of 1530.

➡ The eclectic Juliusz Słowacki Theatre (modelled on the Paris Opéra); the Gothic Holy Cross Church.

The oldest and most interesting of the Jagellonian University's buildings is Collegium Maius, which has been in its possession since 1400 (before that date teaching was probably conducted at Wawel Castle). It came into being when several older houses were joined together. In 1492-1497, it received a beautiful, late Gothic arcaded courtyard with diamond vaults. Further enlarged in Renaissance style, the building was subsequently re-modelled during the 19th and 20th centuries, acquiring historicist features. In 1860, the priceless Jagellonian Library collection was moved there. The building was restored to its original shape in 1949-1964 and is now the seat of the University Museum and houses part of the Art History Institute. The halls of Collegium Maius still serve the needs of the academic community: the University Senate holds its meetings in the library, while the *Stuba Communis* (or Common Room) is where the University's Rectors are elected. Inscribed on the wall of the *Aula* (Assembly Hall) is the University's motto: *Plus ratio quam vis*. The Museum's exhibits include the rectorial insignia: sceptres, rings and chains. There is also a unique collection of old astronomical instruments (with an Arabian astrolabe from 1054), laboratory equipment and globes (the 16th-century Jagellonian Globe is the first globe to show America).

Around the corner from Collegium Maius stands the monumental collegiate church of St. Anne, whose history has been inextricably linked to that of the university. The first house of worship was built on this site as early as the 14th century. Gradually enlarged, it underwent complete remodelling towards the end of the 17th century, to the design of the outstanding architect Tylman van Gameren. At that time, it already enjoyed the status of a collegiate church, enhanced by the relics of St. John of Kanti (a Jagellonian University professor) that were kept there. In the years 1689-1703, van Gameren, the stucco decorator Baldassare Fontana, and the painter Karl Danquart created one of the greatest works of Polish Baroque. The lavishly decorated interior contains many elements emphasising the links between the church and the University.

Opposite the St Anne's is the Nowodworski College, which used to house the first secondary school in Poland, established in 1588 by the Cracow Academy.

1. Collegium Maius, the Stuba Communis.
2. Rectorial sceptres, late 15th cent.
3. Interior of St. Anne's Church.

➡ The diminutive Reformati church and monastery, in the crypt of which rest the mummified corpses of monks and benefactors of the monastery.

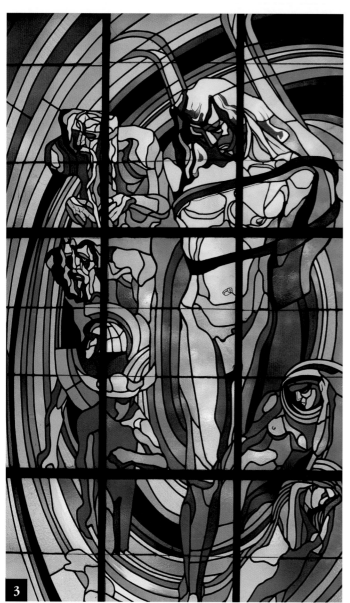

CRACOW

Cracow is not a mere repository of historic monuments: it has always been a melting pot of various intellectual and artistic trends. Art Nouveau, the vibrant artistic movement of the turn of the 19th century, directed against formalised academic and historicist art, found an enthusiastic reception in Cracow. It achieved its fullest form in architecture, interior decoration and craft design.

Art Nouveau style was characterised by the freedom of composition and stylisation, the use of cursive lines and rich ornamentation. The leading exponents of Art Nouveau in Cracow included the writer Stanisław Przybyszewski, and one of the greatest and most versatile Polish artists of all times – Stanisław Wyspiański (1869–1907). A playwright, poet and painter, he aimed at a synthesis of arts. Wyspiański's interests included set design, interior decoration, painting, stained-glass design, book design and murals – and he achieved mastery in all these fields. A good example of Wyspiański's concern for harmony in decorative arts is provided by his decoration of the Franciscan Church interior in Cracow, combining murals and stained-glass windows. The wild flowers painted on the walls are echoed by the motifs appearing in the stained-glass, amid the figures of saints. Another harmonious interior in Art Nouveau style (enriched with folk art themes) is the assembly hall in Cracow's Medical Society building, where Wyspiański designed nearly all the elements: stained-glass decoration, furniture, railings, curtains and tapestries.

The development of Cracovian Art Nouveau owed a great deal to the Polish Applied Art Association, which sought to bring about a revival of arts and crafts in Poland, inspired by Polish folk art and the tradition of the past. Members of the Association (among others, J. Czajkowski, Karol Frycz, Józef Mehoffer, Jan Stanisławski, Stanisław Wyspiański) designed stained-glass windows, furniture, fabrics, ceramics, contributed book and magazine illustrations, and made comprehensive interior designs, for instance, at the Old Theatre, the City Council, or the "Jama Michalika" café. The latter was the venue of the "Green Balloon" literary cabaret (1905–1912), a joint artistic venture of Cracow artists and men of letters. In time, the walls of the café became covered with their paintings and caricatures. Cracovian Art Nouveau can be seen not only in museums, but also in churches. Most striking are the stained glass windows designed by Stanisław Wyspiański (e.g. in the Franciscan Church) and by Józef Mehoffer (e.g. in St. Mary's Church). Thanks to the efforts of the Cracow Stained Glass, Artistic Glazing and Glass Mosaic Studios, Art Nouveau glasswork is still to be seen in the staircases of fashionable buildings from the first years of the 20th century. Other collaborators of the Studios included Kazimierz Sichulski and Karol Frycz.

1. Old Theatre façade.
2. Art Nouveau interior decoration of the "Jama Michalika".
3. Apollo Bound or The Copernican System – *stained glass by Wyspiański.*

➡ The Decius Villa of 1535 – a sizeable Renaissance palace, built for the eminent humanist Justus Decius.

Kazimierz received its municipal charter from King Kazimierz the Great in 1335 and remained a separate town for centuries. In the late 15th century, this important crafts centre became home to a prosperous Jewish community. Large numbers of Jews had settled in Poland in the 13th century, fleeing persecution in Western Europe. In 1264, Prince Bolesław the Pious granted the Jewish community the right to establish its own institutions, including courts (acting on the ruler's behalf), and to engage in commerce and usury. These privileges were confirmed by King Kazimierz the Great, who entrusted the management of state finances to Cracow's Jews. The axis of the *Oppidum Iudaeorum* (Jewish town) was today's Szeroka street.

Numerous monuments of Jewish culture can be seen in Kazimierz, including the Old Synagogue (among the oldest in Europe!) built towards the end of the 15th century and reconstructed in 1557-1570 after a fire. During the Second World War, the Nazis robbed the synagogue of all its precious furnishings and destroyed the building itself. Rebuilt in 1955-1959, it now houses a museum devoted to the history and culture of Cracow's Jews. The magnificent interior is covered with a Gothic vault supported on two slender columns of stone. Another interesting sight is the orthodox Remuh synagogue. Founded by Israel Auerbach in 1553, it is still used for religious worship today. Its furnishings include an authentic Renaissance Holy Ark and a money-box. Next to the synagogue is the Renaissance Remuh Cemetery, a pilgrimage spot visited by Jews from all over the world. This old cemetery derives its name from Rabbi Isserles, known as Moses-Remuh, who is buried there. The Rabbi lived in the 15th century, and was the son of the founder of the synagogue. The Remuh Cemetery was likewise devastated by the Nazis, who used the tombstones to pave roads. Fragments of the tombstones salvaged after the war have been embedded in the cemetery wall. As the cemetery was being renovated, another stratum of tombstones was discovered, dating back to the 16th and 17th centuries. This picturesque collection of reliefs and Hebrew inscriptions cannot but inspire tragic reflection: the Jewish inhabitants of Kazimierz were exterminated by the Nazis during the Second World War.

1. Tebam in the Old Synagogue.
2. Tombstones at the Remuh Cemetery.

➡ The Corpus Christi Church (18-metres high early Baroque altar) and adjoining monastery.

CRACOW – TYNIEC

At the point where the Vistula cuts through the rocky outcrops to the West of Cracow, perched atop a steep Jurassic cliff by a bend in the river is the characteristic twin-towered silhouette of the Tyniec Abbey, surrounded by an irregularly shaped wall. For centuries, the imposing façade has towered above the verdant limestone cliff, its reflection caught in the waters of slow-moving river. A solitary hill in what was once a remote and desolate place was fitting scenery in which to implement the idea of distancing oneself from earthly affairs in self-imposed isolation and directing one's thoughts to God. In the past, however, the power of the Tyniec Abbey did not rest solely on the moral ascendancy of the disciples of St. Benedict of Nursia. The munificence of monarchs and benefactors made Tyniec one of the most opulent abbeys in Poland. Founded in 1044 by Prince Kazimierz the Restorer, it must have been a large-scale construction project from the very outset, as evidenced by the preserved Romanesque fragments. During the reign of Bolesław the Wry-mouthed, the Abbey received numerous endowments, and the monks conducted extensive missionary and commercial activities. The existing church was built in the 15th century. However, thorough remodelling in 1618-1622 and in the early 19th century changed its original appearance. From the 17th century, the lucrative position of abbot was given by Polish kings to their protégés.

In the 19th century, the order was suppressed by the Austrian government, and the abbey buildings (except the church) fell into ruin. After secularisation, the immense treasures of the abbey were dispersed. Their greater part ended up in Tarnów, where the last abbot of Tyniec became the first bishop of the newly-established diocese. Restored in 1939, the Benedictines have lived in Tyniec to this day. A visit to the Abbey is well worth the effort, if only to hear the chorales sung by the monks and to admire the panoramic view. The craggy ruins visible at the edge of the cliff are a memento of an extremely rare phenomenon in Poland: towards the end of the 18th century, the upper parts of the walls and part of the cliff plunged into the river during an earthquake.

1. The Benedictine Abbey at Tyniec.
2. The Abbey Church at Tyniec.

➡ The medieval Cistercian church and monastery in Mogiła adjoins the district of Nowa Huta, built in accordance with the town-planning principles of Socialist Realism.

CRACOW – BIELANY

Bielany, a part of the Zwierzyniec district, is famous for the Camaldolese monastery with its hermit lodges. This contemplative order, following the rule of St. Benedict, arrived in Poland in 1604 and established a hermitage on Srebrna Góra ("Silver Mountain") in Bielany, within the Wolski Forest, named after Marshal Mikołaj Wolski, who founded the monastery in 1605. As the Camaldolese rule prescribes total isolation, the monks live reclusive lives within their *claustrum*, staying in separate lodges and devoting their time to prayer, meditation and physical work in their tiny gardens. Except at certain times of day, they are forbidden from talking to one another, and the thought of the inevitability of death is their ever-present companion. The rule also dictates that Camaldolese places of worship should be austere in appearance. This particular point did not find favour with Wolski, who had an enormous church erected in the years 1605-1642, with a broad nave and side chapels, clearly reminiscent of Italian Baroque. The church was designed by the architect Andrea Spezza, although initially the work was supervised by Valentin von Säbisch. The sombre nave contrasts with the chapels, rich in stuccoes and murals, executed by the best Cracovian artists of the day, working under the guidance of the Italian artist Tommaso Dolabella. The founder of the monastery was buried at the entrance to the church, dressed in a monk's habit. The crypt was placed in such a way that anyone entering the church would have to tread on Wolski's epitaph – a gesture of humility quite typical of the Counter Reformation. Neither the hermits' lodges on Srebrna Góra, nor the chapter house and library, are accessible to the public. Women are allowed in the church on only 12 days during the year. The monastery on Srebrna Góra is one of the best examples of harmony between architecture and landscape to be found in Poland. Time seems to stand still here. In a nearby Austrian fort (called "Skała"), the Jagellonian University has its astronomical observatory.

1. Hermit lodges at the Bielany monastery.
2. Ceiling of the monastery church.

➡ The forts of the Cracow fortress, built in the 19th century – a remarkable complex of fortifications illustrating the changes in military thought.

WIELICZKA

A short distance from Cracow lies the small town of Wieliczka. Salt had been obtained there ten centuries before the Polish state came into being, and the extraction of that commodity on a regular basis has been documented since the end of the 13th century. The history of Wieliczka has been inextricably connected with the unique salt mine. The very name of the place in its Latin form – *Magna Sal* ("Great Salt") reflected the very special position occupied by that mineral in the life of the town. In the 14th century, Wieliczka became one of the chief mining centres in Poland and Europe (it had received its municipal charter before 1290).

The extraction and distribution of salt was handled by the saltworks, owned by the king and managed by an appointed official known as a *żupnik* (*zupparius* in Latin). This was a major and steady source of revenue for the Crown. An ordinance issued by King Kazimierz the Great in 1368 regulated the operation of the Cracow saltworks. Wieliczka has long attracted visitors; however, venturing into the mine down the miners' shafts was fraught with danger. In 1744, steps were hewn in the rock to allow visitors easier access.

Nowadays, the extraction of salt from the giant labyrinth of chambers and galleries has all but finished, and the mine itself is a tourist destination. The Saltworks Museum housed in the heavily remodelled Gothic castle from the reign of King Kazimierz the Great organises breathtaking underground tours for visitors. Access is restricted to the three upper levels of the mine, but even so a depth of 135 metres can be reached. The mine boasts underground lakes, chambers filled with stalactites, and reconstructed old mining equipment, such as hauling gear.

The most interesting parts of the mine include two chapels hewn out of salt, dedicated to St. Anthony and St. Kinga. Off bounds for tourists is the Crystal Cave – an 80-metre high natural wonder, protected as a geological reserve. Since 1964, the mine's microclimate has been used in the treatment of respiratory tract diseases. The Wieliczka mine has been included on UNESCO's World Heritage List.

1. Old-type hauling equipment.
2. The Blessed Kinga Chapel in the Wieliczka salt mine.

➡ Nowy Wiśnicz, the Lubomirski Castle; Bochnia, the salt mine; Niepołomice Forest – a large area of woodland at the confluence of the Vistula and Raba rivers.

AUSCHWITZ

In the town of Oświęcim on the border of Silesia lies one of the most distressing and shocking sites in Europe – Auschwitz, the largest Nazi death camp and a place of mass murder. The passing time will never dampen the feeling of utter horror experienced by visitors as they pass through the gate with its cynical motto: *Arbeit macht frei*, walk past the ruined crematoria, peek into the prisoners' huts.

The camp was set up in May 1940 upon the orders of Heinrich Himmler, in Zasole, an Oświęcim suburb incorporated at that time into the Third Reich. In October 1941, Auschwitz II – Birkenau (Brzezinka), a new subdivision of Auschwitz for 200,000 prisoners was created. The camp was manned by ca. 6,000 SS officers. The first transports of Polish political prisoners commenced in mid-1940. Apart from Poland, people were dispatched to Auschwitz from some 30 other countries. The most numerous groups were Soviet prisoners of war, Gypsies, and above all Jews. Auschwitz became a mass killing ground for Jews from all over Europe; extermination was carried out by means of Zyklon-B poison gas. The prisoners were used as slave labour by the German war industry, including such concerns as IG Farben, Krupp and others.

All told, no less than 1.2 million prisoners, the vast majority of them Jews, perished in Auschwitz through backbreaking labour and mass extermination. Piles of spectacles, shoes, toys, and hair today bear silent witness to this unspeakable tragedy.

Auschwitz was also the place of the martyrdom of Father Maksymilian Kolbe (1894-1941), a Franciscan friar who volunteered to take the place of a fellow prisoner who was condemned to be starved to death in retribution for the escape of another prisoner. Father Kolbe was canonised in 1982.

When the Soviet army liberated the camp in January 1945, only 7,500 prisoners were found alive.

1. The gate to Auschwitz-Birkenau.
2. Guard tower at Auschwitz.

➡ Pszczyna: The Promnitz and Hochberg Castle and Park – now a museum of interior decoration and design.

KALWARIA ZEBRZYDOWSKA

Among the most precious historical relics of Małopolska, whose importance transcends regional and national boundaries, is the Kalwaria Zebrzydowska pilgrimage site, included on UNESCO's World Heritage List. This architectural complex, comprising the Bernardine Church and the Via Dolorosa chapels, spread out over a wooded hill, is a magnificent work of art which remains to this day a centre of fervent religious cult. The origin of Kalwaria goes back to the year 1600, when the Palatine of Cracow Mikołaj Zebrzydowski decided to build a Holy Cross Chapel there, modelled on the Holy Sepulchre Chapel in Jerusalem. The cornerstone was laid in 1603. In 1604-1617, a monastery, church and large group of chapels arose in the beautiful Beskidy Mountain landscape. After Mikołaj Zebrzydowski's death in 1620, the work was continued by his son Jan.

The church and monastery buildings were designed by the Jesuit architect Gianmaria Bernardoni. At the turn of the 17th century, the church was enlarged with the addition of a spacious nave and a twin-towered façade. Among the rich, Baroque interior decorations is a venerated image of the Madonna and Child. There is an interesting double-sided, open-work high altar of 1723, separating the chancel and the monks' choir – an exquisite example of Baroque wood-carving. In the monks' choir behind the altar, there are fine stalls decorated with scenes from the life of the Blessed Virgin Mary and a Mannerist ornament.

Today, the Kalwaria complex consists of the basilican monastery church and 42 Calvary chapels that recreate the appearance of Jerusalem 2000 years ago. The chapels are the venue for traditional religious services and provide the setting for the annual Passion play performed during Easter Week, and the Triumph of the Blessed Virgin Mary on the Feast of the Assumption. The Marian processions at Kalwaria belong to the most spectacular religious events in Poland. The pilgrimage tradition at Kalwaria remains very much alive despite the rapid pace of change in the world.

1. A Calvary chapel.
2. "Paradise Square" in front of the Kalwaria Zebrzydowska church.

➡ Mogilany – the Renaissance park of the Jordan family residence amid the hilly landscape of the Beskidy; Sucha Beskidzka – the Renaissance castle and an old inn.

WADOWICE

Although the oldest source mentioning the town of Wadowice dates back to 1327, and the town itself boasts a picturesque market square and an 18th-century parish church, it is known today primarily as the birthplace of Pope John Paul II. The house where the Holy Father was born is now a museum devoted to his life and work. Karol Wojtyła was born in Wadowice in 1920. In 1938, he took up Polish studies at the Jagiellonian University, interrupted by the outbreak of the Second World War. In 1942, he began to study at the University's underground Theology Faculty. Ordained in 1946, Father Wojtyła continued his theological studies in Rome, where he obtained a doctorate in theology in 1948. In 1964, he was appointed Archbishop of Cracow and in 1947 became a cardinal. He took an active part in the Second Vatican Council. After the death of Pope John Paul I, he was elected Pope on 16 October 1978 and assumed the name of John Paul II. His election created a worldwide sensation and was seen as an event of not only religious, but also political significance. John Paul II has been carrying on the work of his great predecessors, John XXIII and Paul VI. Papal visits to countries in every corner of the world have become the hallmark of his pontificate. He has visited Poland seven times: in 1979, 1983, 1987, 1991, 1997, 1999 and, briefly, in 1995, on the occasion of a trip to Slovakia. The pilgrimage of 1979 was particularly momentous. The great impact of the Pope's message and the people's tremendous response shook the self-confidence of the communist authorities. It was the first time after the war that Poles had a chance to display their national dignity in public, destroying the myth of their alleged "attachment to socialism". At the heart of the Pope's teaching is Man – in an inextricable relationship with God – his dignity and his rights. John Paul II has led the Catholic world into the year 2000 – the great millennium. He has written several collections of verse, published mostly under the pen name of Andrzej Jawień, meditative religious poems and plays, and an influential book published in 1994 –*Crossing the Threshold of Hope.*

1. *John Paul II in his home town.*
2. *Façade of the parish church.*

➡ Żywiec – castle in a formal garden; Szczyrk – a winter resort; Barania Góra – the source of the Vistula River.

THE PRĄDNIK VALLEY

The Prądnik Valley is an area abounding in natural wonders and cultural landmarks. Merely 17 km long, it contains a mass of rare geomorphological features, including some 210 caves (the most famous being the Łokietek Cavern and the Ciemna ("Dark") Cave) and peculiar rock formations with lots of limestone needles (e.g. the "Club of Hercules"), and is extraordinarily rich in flora. Its vegetation includes a fair number of relict species. One of the local peculiarities is the giant puffball, one of the largest fungi of the world. As regards the animal world, the area is home to a large population of bats. In 1956, the Ojców National Park (Poland's smallest) was established here. The cultural legacy of the region is equally diverse, ranging from prehistoric settlements (Ogrojec, next to the Ciemna Cave, the forts on Okopy Hill, at Sułoszowa and at Grodzisko) to castles (in Pieskowa Skała and Ojców), places of worship (the hermitage of the Blessed Salomea at Grodzisko) and the old spa facilities at Ojców (numerous villas from the turn of the 19th century). Besides, there are remnants of old water mills, powder magazines, fulling mills and sawmills (at the high point of industrial development in the Prądnik Valley, there were over 60 establishments in operation).

But the most notable manmade object in the valley (apart from the castle ruins at Ojców with a 50-metre deep well sunk in rock) is the fortified residence at Pieskowa Skała. The castle was founded by Kazimierz the Great, but it soon passed into the hands of the powerful Szafraniec family, in whose possession it remained until the early 17th century. Remodelled in Renaissance style, the castle became one of the most beautiful residences in Małopolska. Unfortunately, it suffered considerable destruction at the hands of the Swedish invaders in 1655 and 1702. Even so, it has always attracted attention of visitors on account of its scenic location. Thoroughly restored after the Second World War, it now functions as a museum – a branch of the Wawel collections. The castle, as well as the entire Prądnik Valley and its caves, have given rise to many romantic legends.

1. Prądnik Valley: Pieskowa Skała Castle with the "Club of Hercules" at its foot.
2. The Renaissance castle at Pieskowa Skała.

➡ Krzeszowice – a 19th century spa with the Potocki Palace surrounded by a large park; Rudno – the picturesque ruins of Tęczyn Castle.

MODLNICA

The manor house – once the abode of the landed gentry, extolled in literature – is perhaps the most characteristically Polish type of residence, noted for its specific structural features and unpretentious appearance. An early manor house was typically a one-storey timber building with a shingled roof. Its interior would be divided into a kitchen, bedrooms and a common room (knights' hall). The size, layout, decoration and furnishings depended on the wealth of the owner. In the 16th century, some manor houses were already built of brick. At the same time, annexes began to appear at the corners and the roof assumed the characteristic "Polish mansard" form. Many of the old manors, thanks to their suitable location and surrounding ramparts or solid fences with gates, served a defensive function. Later on, the design of the Polish manor house bore a visible imprint of Classicism.

This architectural form is beautifully exemplified by the manor house at Modlnica on the outskirts of Cracow. From the late Middle Ages, the estate belonged to several wealthy patrician families, in 1782 coming into the possession of the Konopkas. In its present form, the manor house dates back to the latter half of the 18th century. The columned portico with a triangular pediment in front and columns *in antis* at the back, the façade decoration, and the high mansard roof make it an outstanding example of the traditional Polish manor house. The surrounding park, with a terraced layout and magnificent old trees, dates back to the Renaissance in its oldest parts.

Towards the end of the 19th century, the Modlnica manor house was a favourite meeting place of Cracow's cultural and intellectual elite. Among the guests were the painter Artur Grottger, the folklorist Oskar Kolberg, and, in 1905, Włodzimierz Tetmajer, the painter of the polychrome decoration in the small parish church nearby. Today, the manor house serves as a reception centre for the Rector of the Jagiellonian University. It thus serves once again as a meeting place of the elites.

1. *Ceiling painting in the 18th-cent. Laskowa manor.*
2. *The manor house at Modlnica.*

➡ Jurassic valleys near Cracow – an ideal place for rock-climbing; Czerna – the Discalced Carmelite monastery.

CZĘSTOCHOWA

"A tempera painting on a panel made of three linden planks lined with canvas, enclosed in a profiled Gothic frame, 1215 × 815 mm, representing the Madonna and Child; of Byzantine/Ruthenian provenance and uncertain attribution and date." This dry conservator's description does not even pretend to account for the significance of the Black Madonna to the Polish nation, for the nationwide character of the Marian cult, and for the flocks of pilgrims who walk from the remotest corners of Poland to the Częstochowa shrine each year.

The pious tradition of making pilgrimages to Jasna Góra, the site of the Black Madonna shrine, is as old as the Pauline monastery itself, established by Duke Władysław II of Opole, who in 1382 invited Pauline monks from Hungary to settle in Poland. He endowed them with a hill near Częstochowa and soon after had a miraculous icon of the Madonna brought to the monastery from Red Ruthenia (possibly via Hungary). According to legend, the image was painted by St. Luke the Evangelist himself, on planks from the table at which the Holy Family had prayed and dined.

The latest research reveals that the icon dates from the 13th century and was initially placed in an iconostasis somewhere in the Balkans. Many of the faithful, particularly in the 17th and 18th centuries, viewed the Częstochowa icon as one of the most venerable Christian relics – on a par with such images of Christ "not made by human hand" as the Turin Shroud, the Mandilion of Edessa or the Cloth of St. Veronica. In 1430, the icon was desecrated by the Hussites. On Easter Day, the attackers looted the monastery, took away the precious furnishings, and dropped the icon outside the church – robbed of its precious cover and votive offerings and broken into three parts. That event left visible scars – two parallel cuts – on the Madonna's face, which were purposefully left untouched as the painting underwent renovation in 15th-century Cracow, at the expense of King Władysław Jagiełło (the earliest documented conservation work in Poland!).

1. *The Black Madonna icon.*
2. *The Miraculous Icon Chapel.*
3. *Jasna Góra Monastery, Częstochowa.*

➡ Piotrków Trybunalski – the Old Town with a castle and churches; Sulejów – the old Cistercian monastery; Gidle – the Dominican Church.

The architectural complex on Jasna Góra gradually evolved over the centuries. The church was built in 1460-1463 and it was approximately at the same time that the Miraculous Icon Chapel was constructed in the former cloister. This is the destination for the countless pilgrims who visit the monastery. The chapel was enlarged in 1641-1644 on the initiative of Bishops Stanisław and Maciej Łubieński, as the old Gothic chapel could not hold all the faithful. In 1650, the chapel received an imposing retable donated by the Grand Chancellor of the Crown, Jerzy Ossoliński. It was made of oak, lined with ebony and silver. The icon itself was given a magnificent repoussé silver cover.

The chapel adjoins the church building, remodelled in 1690-1693 in a Baroque spirit. The tower was built in 1600-1620, and in 1699-1703 raised to its present height of 106 metres (there are as many as 519 steps leading to the top). Many more chapels were added, too, the most beautiful of which was founded by the Denhoff family in 1644-1671. The monastery building was likewise given its present form in the 17th century.

Jasna Góra was also a stronghold. According to common belief, the cuts on the Black Madonna's face were inflicted by Swedish soldiers. However, this rather naive interpretation ignores the historical facts: the six-week siege of Jasna Góra by the Swedes in 1655 ended with the unconditional retreat of the invaders, and Prior Augustyn Kordecki, who commanded the defence of the monastery, has been regarded as a national hero ever since, while the event itself has become one of the prominent motifs in Polish patriotic tradition. The bastion-type fortifications built after 1620 were remodelled on several occasions. In the second half of the 18th century, they provided shelter for members of the patriotic Confederation of Bar.

Other parts of the shrine, frequently visited by both pilgrims and tourists, include the basilica and its tower, the Knights' Hall, St. Mary's Hall, the Arsenal, the treasuries, the Jasna Góra rampart with the Stations of the Cross, the Chapel of the Last Supper, and the museums with exquisite works of art and votive offerings. Jasna Góra has been included on UNESCO's World Heritage List.

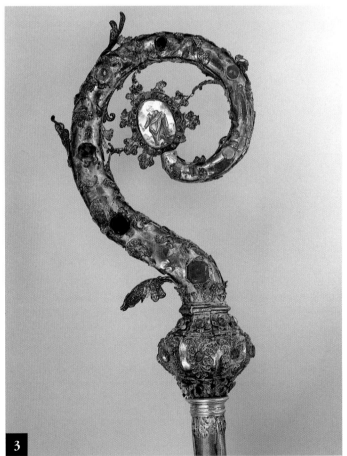

1. *The monastery sacristy.*
2. *The Black Madonna's Ruby Robe.*
3. *Prior Moszkowski's crosier.*

➡ Tarnowskie Góry – a museum of mining technology in an old silver mine; The Błędowska Desert – a large sandy stretch near the town of Klucze.

OGRODZIENIEC

From Częstochowa to Cracow, along the picturesque Jurassic uplands speckled with rocky outcrops, runs a trail of mighty ruins. The "Eagles' Nests", which once guarded the Polish borderlands, have never ceased to impress the onlooker as silent monuments to past splendour. Perhaps the most majestic of these is at Ogrodzieniec.

Ogrodzieniec Castle was built in 1530-1545 for Seweryn Boner, the Burgrave of Cracow and a trusted advisor to King Zygmunt the Old, succeeding an older stronghold from the turn of the 14th century. Boner was a banker of Alsatian descent who made a swift career in Poland. The King's favour and family connections brought him a position of rank among the richest magnates. He had a residence built which, with its numerous towers, deliberately mimicked medieval castles, and it was only the irregular shape of the inner courtyard and the form of some of the fortifications that betrayed the castle's more modern provenance. Its construction and remodelling was continued by Seweryn's son Stanisław.

The castle came under attack several times. It was first captured in 1587 by the troops of Archduke Maximilian, the Habsburg pretender to the Polish throne. During the Swedish invasion in the latter half of the 17th century, known as the "Deluge", the residence was captured. Somewhat unusually, however, the Swedes did not cause any significant destruction to the castle. After the war, it was restored by the new owner, Stanisław Warszycki, who had it surrounded by an outer wall with a gate and a drawbridge. It was only in 1702 that the castle suffered severe damage, when it was set on fire by the Swedish troops of King Charles XII. Afterwards, it gradually fell into ruin, and in the early 19th century local people began to dismantle its walls for building materials. The sombre ruins gave rise to local legends about a monstrous dog guarding hidden treasure. The place inspired Aleksander Janowski to establish the Polish Tourist Society in 1906. Conservation work, aimed at preserving the ruins in their existing state and making them accessible to the public, was commenced in 1949 and completed in 1973.

1. *The ruins of Ogrodzieniec Castle.*
2. *The Boner Palace at Ogrodzieniec.*

➡ Medieval castle ruins at Bobolice, Mirów and Olsztyn; Potok Złoty – 19th-cent. Krasiński Palace housing a museum of the poet Zygmunt Krasiński.

WIŚLICA

The name Wiślica evokes associations with Poland's earliest history and the Vistulanian state of which it was the hypothetical capital. Beyond any doubt, it was one of the more significant centres of the Piast period. Not far from the market square, at the site of the former castle, are relics of an early Piast palatium and an 11th-century chapel. The Piast castle was destroyed by the Tartars in 1241, but Kazimierz the Great had it rebuilt and surrounded the town with walls. In 1347, the first codified body of laws in Polish history – the Wiślica Statutes – was compiled here. In 1657, Wiślica was destroyed by the Swedes, and in the 18th century, the ruined castle was pulled down. Fortunately, an interesting Gothic collegiate church with a double nave has been preserved. Below the original vaults supported on slender pillars, the unpretentious high altar contains a figure from ca. 1300, known as "Łokietek's Madonna" – associated with King Władysław the Elbow-High.

Excavations carried out in the collegiate church in 1959-1972 revealed relics of a Romanesque church from the second half of the 12th century and a crypt with a now famous floor slab bearing engraved figural scenes, which has been dated to 1166-1177. The surviving fragment is divided into two fields, enclosed in a border incorporating floral and animal motifs. In either field, three figures are shown in prayer. An inscription explains what the depicted members of the princely family are praying for: "We desire to be trodden upon so that we might ascend to the stars one day." Bearing in mind the high status of the alleged founder, Prince Kazimierz the Just, the Wiślica slab is proof of the ruler's exceptional humility in the face of God. The conservation work also uncovered Byzantine-Ruthenian polychrome decoration commissioned by King Władysław Jagiełło.

In the vicinity of the church are a late-Gothic belfry and a vicarage founded by the famous 15th-century chronicler Jan Długosz (1415-1480) – Canon of Cracow, royal tutor and chronicler, regarded as Poland's first historian.

1. *The Collegiate Church in Wiślica.*
2. *Romanesque floor slab, 12th cent.*
3. *Founding tablet of the Collegiate Church in Wiślica.*

➡ Zalipie – a centre of folk painting with richly adorned houses; Pińczów – the main centre of the Polish Brethren sect during the Reformation, with a beautiful market square.

JĘDRZEJÓW

In 1140-1149, Janik Gryfita, the future archbishop of Gniezno, founded in Jędrzejów the first Cistercian abbey in Poland. The monks came from Morimond in Burgundy. It was in the Jędrzejów monastery that Bishop Wincenty Kadłubek (1150?-1223), a renowned chronicler, chaplain and secretary to Prince Kazimierz the Just, spent the final years of his life. As Cracow Bishop (appointed in 1208) he took part in the Fourth Lateran Council (1215). In 1218, he voluntarily renounced his office and went to live in the monastery. His chronicle was divided into four parts. The last one covered the reign of Mieszko the Old and Kazimierz the Just (until 1202). He gave a vivid, if tendentious account of the controversy between Bishop Stanisław Szczepanowski and King Bolesław the Bold (as a result of which the Bishop died a martyr's death and the King was forced into exile). His version of the story made an indirect contribution to the Bishop's canonisation in 1253.

The monastic church, despite undergoing Baroque remodelling in the 18th century, has retained its Romanesque layout and detail from the early 13th century, with Gothic elements added in the second half of the 15th century. The twin-towered, late Baroque façade, which provides the dominant accent in the landscape of Jędrzejów, was built in 1751-1754. Inside, the decoration comprises Baroque polychrome painting from 1734-1739 and sculptures from the Cracow workshop of Antoni Frąckiewicz (first half of the 18th century). The church, with a fine 54-voice organ, is regularly used as a venue for music festivals attracting large numbers of music lovers. The monastery buildings originate from the latter half of the 15th century and from the 18th century.

Jędrzejów is also home to Poland's largest collection of clocks and astronomical instruments – 480 exhibits in all – including a sundial collection believed to be the third biggest in the world (next to Oxford and Chicago). It originated as a private collection of the Przypkowski family, who donated it to the state in 1962. Apart from clocks, it includes first editions of works by Copernicus, Galileo and Kepler.

1. The Cistercian abbey at Jędrzejów.
2. Nave of the monastic church in Jędrzejów.
3. Organ at the Cistercian abbey, 18th cent.

➡ Tokarnia – open-air museum of regional architecture; Busko Zdrój – spa and park; Chęciny – 13th-century castle.

KIELCE

Already at the end of the 11th century, Kielce belonged to the Cracow bishops, from whom it also received its charter in 1364. The most valuable historical monument in the town is the impressive, early Baroque Bishops' Palace, erected for Bishop Jakub Zadzik in 1637-1641. The identity of the designer is not certain, as Tomasso Poncino, whose name appears in the archives, was more a mason than an architect – hence the conjectural attribution of the Palace to the royal architect Giovanni Trevano.

Bishop Zadzik commissioned the best painter of his time, Tommaso Dolabella, to portray the most important events in which he had participated as Grand Chancellor of the Crown: the conclusion of the treaty with Sweden, the imprisonment of Tsar Vasily Shuisky, or the expulsion of the Arians from Poland. Enlarged in the 18th century, the Palace now houses a museum with a fine collection of historical portraits, furniture and arts and crafts. Particularly impressive is the upstairs dining hall, decorated with several dozen portraits of Cracow bishops and metropolitans.

Equally important is the early Baroque cathedral of 1632-1635 – formerly a collegiate church – with rich 18th-century furnishings. The basilica, which superseded an earlier church built on the same site, has impressive Baroque interior decoration; the best woodcarving originates from the workshop of the Cracow master Antoni Frąckiewicz. In 1729, an arcaded passageway connected the Cathedral with the Bishops' Palace.

On the outskirts of Kielce lies an interesting Bernardine complex at Karczówka (1624-1631), while a number of notable buildings from the turn of the 19th century can be seen in the city centre. From the 15th century onwards, the town was associated with ore extraction and metallurgy, and in 1816 the famous geologist Stanisław Staszic established there an Academic School of Mining. It was in Kielce that the writer Stefan Żeromski (1864-1925) attended secondary school – Kielce, disguised in his writings under the telling name of Obrzydłówek ("Abhorrentville"), was for him a symbol of parochialism. Of course, things have changed for the better since Żeromski's day.

1. The Bishops' Palace in Kielce.
2. Baroque interior of the Cathedral.
3. Bartek – an ancient oak-tree at Bartków near Kielce.

➡ Samsonów – ruins of a 19th-cent. ironworks; Oblęgorek – manor house of the writer Henryk Sienkiewicz; Sielpia Wielka – historic rolling mill.

1

2

ŚWIĘTY KRZYŻ

The Świętokrzyskie Mountain range – composed of ancient hills, not too tall, but with steep slopes, abundant rocky outcrops and deep valleys – has for centuries been home to monks, artists, mystics and partisans. Overgrown with age-old fir forest interspersed with stony screes, it cradles at its very heart the famous shrine where a particle from the Holy Cross used to be venerated. At the foot of the hill the mysterious stone figure of a pilgrim supposedly ascends Święty Krzyż (Holy Cross) Hill at a rate of one grain of sand per year. When it reaches the hilltop sanctuary, the world will come to an end. In pre-Christian days, the hill the stone pilgrim is headed for (also known as Łysa Góra, or "Bald Mountain") was a major centre of pagan cult in Poland (8th-10th centuries).

On top of Święty Krzyż is a Benedictine abbey, established in the early 12th century by King Bolesław the Wry-mouthed. Initially, it was dedicated to the Holy Trinity, but from the 13th century onwards, the abbey came to be known under the name of the "Holy Cross", reflecting the spreading cult of the priceless relic kept there. Among the pilgrims was King Władysław Jagiełło himself. It also became the burial place of Prince Jeremi Wiśniowiecki, the nemesis of the Cossacks in the 17th century. This is also where the oldest preserved text of Polish prose originated – the 14th-century *Święty Krzyż Sermons*, consisting of five excerpts and one sermon preserved in full. The sermons deal with church holidays: the author pondered scholastic questions, adding a liberal measure of allegorical commentary. The text clearly shows a concern for the beauty of the language, reflected in the rhythmic structure and ample use of rhyme. In 1819, the abbey was dissolved and its buildings converted into a formidable prison.

The Świętokrzyska Forest contains nearly all the tree species found in Poland, with a predominance of fir and Polish larch. The mountain range is the site of a national park (established in 1950), several dozen reserves and two areas of protected landscape. Apart from the forest, the main attraction of the park are the screes made up of huge boulders.

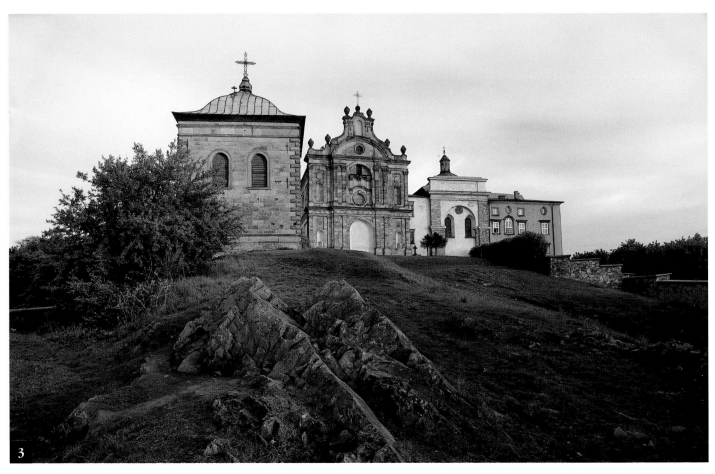

3

1. The Świętokrzyskie Mountains.
2. Old monastery building at Święty Krzyż.
3. Święty Krzyż abbey.

➡ Święta Katarzyna monastery at the foot of Łysica Hill; Nowa Słupia – "Dymarki" archaeological festival, featuring a reconstruction of prehistoric iron-smelting techniques.

UJAZD

Before Louis XIV set out to build his residence at Versailles, Krzyżtopór Castle was said to be – with some exaggeration, to be sure – the largest and most luxurious palace in Europe. Krzysztof Ossoliński, the Palatine of Sandomierz, had a *palazzo in fortezza* built in the village of Ujazd, to bear witness to the power and affluence of his family. The residence was named Krzyżtopór. Two immense reliefs symbolising the castle's name were placed on either side of the marble gate: the cross (*Krzyż*) as a sign of faith, and the hatchet (*topór*) as a symbol embodied in the Ossoliński coat of arms. The earliest document indicating that the castle was inhabited dates from the beginning of 1627. Construction work, which allegedly carried a price-tag of 30 million zlotys, was completed in 1644, under Lorenzo Senes, the court architect of the Ossolińskis. As regards the supposed symbolism of the design, with the four towers standing for the four seasons, 12 halls representing the 12 months of the year, 52 chambers – the 52 weeks in a year, and 365 windows – the 365 days of the year, this was yet another spurious story, which, however, does not detract from the grandeur of the castle. One more Krzyżtopór legend speaks of an immense dining hall whose ceiling took the form of a vast aquarium with iridescent fish swimming right above the guests' heads for their entertainment.

The stone castle consisted of the palace, auxiliary buildings and a system of bastion-type fortifications. A large and well-tended park abutted on the residence. The castle complex was built on a regular, pentagonal plan of the new Italian type. It was 120 metres long and 95 metres wide. The Ossolińskis had little more than ten years in which to enjoy their tremendous mansion. After Krzysztof's death, the palace passed to his son Krzysztof Baldwin, and then Krzyżtopór became the property of the Denhoff and Kalinowski families. In 1655, it was captured by the Swedes, who occupied it on and off until 1657, when they finally burnt it to the ground. Thereafter, no one had the means to restore it to a usable condition, and ever since it has remained a monument to past glory and human vanity.

1. A bird's eye view of Krzyżtopór Castle at Ujazd.
2. The ruins of Krzyżtopór Castle.
3. Krzyżtopór – walls and gates.

➡ Klimontów – a collegiate church with stuccoes by G. Falconi, and the Dominican monastery, founded in the 17th cent. by the Ossoliński family.

OPATÓW

St. Martin's Collegiate Church in Opatów is one of the best preserved and most spectacular Romanesque buildings in Małopolska. This is not to say that it has survived intact in its original 12th-century shape. However, subsequent additions did not destroy the external appearance of this monumental church built of ashlars, with a twin-towered westwork and a transept terminating in apses. The original layout has been preserved in its entirety. Graceful biforate windows, characteristic of the mid-12th century, contribute to a sense of lightness. Inside, there are late Gothic net vaults, while the decoration reveals a Baroque spirit, seen, for instance, in the mid-18th-century murals. Special attention is due to a work known as the *Opatów Lament*. It is part of the tomb of Krzysztof Szydłowiecki, Grand Chancellor of the Crown and a benefactor of the church, erected in 1532–1541 by two artists who had previously contributed to the construction of the Zygmunt Chapel in Cracow's Wawel Cathedral: Bernardino Zanobi de Gianotis and Giovanni Cini. The sizeable stone monument is lined with bronze castings: a plaque with an effigy of the deceased and a tablet placed underneath, showing courtiers and servants mourning his death.

Another attraction of Opatów is the underground tourist route, several hundred metres long, which leads through old cellars and merchants' warehouses. The passages are spread over three levels, the bottom one reaching a depth of 14 metres. Across the Opatówka river is a Bernardine monastery with the Baroque Church of the Blessed Virgin Mary. Also worthy of mention are the Renaissance Warsaw Gate with remnants of the medieval city walls. These were built by Chancellor Krzysztof Szydłowiecki, who bought Opatów from the Lublin Chapter in 1514. Every year in May, the town bustles with excitement during the Opatów Fair, frequented by many folk artists and ensembles.

1. *The collegiate church in Opatów.*
2. *The Szydłowiecki tomb.*
3. *Detail of the* Opatów *Lament.*

➡ Krzemionki – a unique, prehistoric flint mine with a tourist route; the town of Szydłów with its preserved medieval walls.

WĄCHOCK

Wąchock is probably the best preserved Cistercian abbey in Poland, and one of the most precious architectural monuments of the transition period between Romanesque and Gothic. The Wąchock abbey was established by the Cracow Bishop Gedko in 1179, but it was only in 1218–1239 that the stone buildings were erected. Work was supervised by a Master Simon, who inscribed his name on the church façade – it is thus the oldest structure in Poland that can be attributed to a named architect. At that time, a pillared basilica was built, with a transept and a rectangular chancel flanked by two chapels. The architectural and sculptural forms conform to the austere precepts of a rule which prohibited all kinds of extravagance and ostentation. In the 13th century, the abbey was twice destroyed by the Tartar invaders, but privileges granted by Prince Bolesław the Chaste allowed it to be restored. The adjacent monastery with a cloister was heavily remodelled in Baroque style, but inside, one of the most beautiful Romanesque interiors in Poland has survived: the chapter house with a rib vault supported on four columns, whose capitals are adorned with geometric and floral ornamentation. Also worth seeing are the refectory and fraternity hall. Over the centuries, the Cistercian monks reclaimed land in the swampy Kamianna Valley, and organised the extraction and smelting of iron ore.

After many years of prosperity, the town suffered total destruction at the hands of Prince George Rakocsi's troops in 1657. In the first half of the 19th century, Wąchock and the entire Kamianna Valley became an important industrial centre; most of the establishments were destroyed by the Germans during the Second World War. There are other reminders of those tragic times in Wąchock, too. Buried in the cloister is the hero of the Świętokrzyskie Mountains, Major Jan Piwnik "Ponury", the legendary Polish partisan commander. Parachuted in from England, he took command of a large partisan force, which operated from the famous Fir Forest.

1. The Cistercian abbey at Wąchock.
2. The monastery's chapter house.

➡ *Wykus* – a former Home Army partisan camp; *Szydłowiec* – the Museum of Musical Instruments; *Orońsko* – the Centre for Polish Sculpture.

1. Town panorama from across the Vistula.
2. Sandomierz Town Hall.
3. The Piszczele loess ravine.

➡ Ćmielów – the famous chinaware factory; Gościeradów Ukazowy – the neo-classical Prażmowski Palace.

SANDOMIERZ

Situated on the high bank of the Vistula lies Sandomierz – one of Poland's oldest towns and a principality capital during the Fragmentation Period in the Middle Ages. Its development was periodically interrupted by recurring attacks of the Tartar hordes. Rebuilt after the invasions and surrounded with walls, Sandomierz became the venue for political congresses of the magnates and clergy. Nowadays, it is one of the most precious architectural complexes in Poland. Its oldest monuments include the Romanesque Church of St. James from the 13th century, the Gothic Cathedral of St Mary and the House of Jan Długosz, now the seat of the Diocese Museum. The Cathedral is decorated with murals commissioned by Władysław Jagiełło and executed by Ruthenian artists in Byzantine style. At the former Dominican Church of St. James, one of the earliest brick structures in Poland, the visitor's attention is immediately drawn to the beautiful portal with ceramic decoration. After a Lithuanian invasion in 1349, the town was rebuilt on a new plan and in a new style. At the centre was a sloping market square (120 × 100 m) – with side streets, burgher houses and a historic 14th-century Town Hall, remodelled in Renaissance style. As the new layout was being created, the various guilds were allocated building lots in different parts of the town – thus, millers would live in one section, tanners in another, weavers in yet another, and so on. Numerous privileges contributed to the prosperity of this merchant town situated on the Vistula. What is left today of the medieval city walls is the Opatów Gate, crowned with a Renaissance parapet. Another beautiful parapet can be seen on top of the former Jesuit Collegium Gostomianum. Underneath the town are well-preserved cellars, which were used as warehouses by the merchants and provided shelter in times of war; now they can be accessed via an underground tourist route. Fragments of the castle built by Kazimierz the Great and converted into a Renaissance mansion, blown up by the Swedes in 1656, have been restored and reconstructed. Sandomierz is situated on loess uplands above the Vistula valley. In places, the town's elevation above the river reaches 65 metres.

1. *Silver ciborium from the Mansionaries Chapel, 1639.*
2. *Sandomierz Cathedral.*

→ Koprzywnica – a former Cistercian monastery with the Church of St. Florian; Tarnobrzeg-Dzików – 19th-cent. Tarnowski Palace.

1. *The Cracow Gate in Lublin.* 2. *The Lubomelski House on the Main Square.* 3. *Street in the Old Town.* 4. *The St. Stanisław Kostka Chapel in the Cathedral.*

➡ Kozłówka – Zamoyski Square (the annexes house a museum of Socialist Realism); swamps, peat bogs and marshes in the Polesie National Park.

LUBLIN

A stronghold existed at the site of today's Lublin already in the 12th century, and an adjacent settlement received its charter in 1317. In 1341, Kazimierz the Great built a castle on the lofty hill to protect the town, which prospered thanks to intensive borderland trade between Poland and Ruthenia. From the end of the 14th century, Lublin enjoyed a *de facto* monopoly on trade between the Crown (i.e., Poland) and Lithuania. It became the scene of one of the most important events in the history of Poland – the Polish-Lithuanian Union signed on 1 July 1569. This provided for one monarch for both countries, a common parliamen , currency and foreign policy. The two countries were to retain separate armies, offices and courts. Thus, the Commonwealth of the Two Nations was born. From 1578, Lublin was the seat of the Crown Tribunal – the supreme court of appeal for the nobility. Any unjust verdicts were supposedly rectified by the devil himself, who left his imprint on the courtroom table. Nowadays, Lublin is the largest administrative, academic and industrial centre in eastern Poland, with five institutions of higher education. The historic layout of the town has been preserved, together with the market square, town hall, sections of the city walls and beautiful houses from the 16th-19th centuries. The castle, which was remodelled in the 17th century, owes its present, neo-Gothic appearance to the architect Jan Stompf, who redesigned it in 1823-1826. The most valuable fragment of the castle is the Gothic chapel with Byzantine-Ruthenian murals from 1418, commissioned by Władysław Jagiełło. Opposite the castle is the Gothic Brama Grodzka ("Town Gate"), once connected to the castle by means of a drawbridge. Across the Old Town is the 14th-century Cracow Gate, at which three routes diverged – towards Warsaw and Cracow, Zamość and Lvov, and the Podlasie lands. Among the churches, especially noteworthy are the former Jesuit Church from the 16th-17th centuries (since 1818 a cathedral), the monasteries of the Dominicans (16th-17th c., with the impressive Firlej Chapel from 1615), Bernardines (16th c.), Discalced Carmelite Nuns (17th c.), Missionaries (17th and 18th c.), and the late Baroque monastery of Calced Carmelites from ca. 1742.

1. *Lublin Castle's Trinity Chapel with Ruthenian-Byzantine murals.*
2. *Lublin Castle.*

➡ Lubartów – an old town with the Palace of the Lubomirski and Sanguszko families; Majdanek – Nazi death camp.

ZAMOŚĆ

Jan Zamoyski (1542–1605) was the closest collaborator of King Stefan Bathory. The offices of Chancellor and Commander-in-Chief brought him an enormous fortune, which allowed him to build a model Renaissance town – an everlasting monument to its founder's vision. He chose a location on the route from the Baltic to the Black Sea. Zamość was founded in 1580; its layout was planned in 1578 by the Italian architect Bernardo Morando, who also designed many of the houses and the fortification system. The fortress-town that thus came into being embodied one of the most creative town planning concepts in Europe at the time. Chancellor Zamoyski's town was built on a pentagonal plan with a grid of streets, an equal-sided Grand Market Square and two other squares – the Water Market and the Salt Market. Tax exemptions, privileges and the security provided by the modern fortifications attracted settlers of many nationalities. Zamość became an important commercial centre. In 1589, it was incorporated into the "Zamoyski Estate" – an indivisible property inherited through primogeniture, in contrast with prevailing customs and laws. Since 1963, the town has been undergoing systematic renovation. One of the greatest attractions of Zamość is its very layout, with fortifications and gates, as well as the Renaissance palace, remodelled in Baroque style. Other magnificent buildings include the imposing collegiate church dedicated to the Resurrection and to St. Thomas the Apostle. The Grand Market Square is a real jewel of Polish Renaissance architecture. The houses along its flanks have retained their original arcades and beautiful external decorations. And the Town Hall protruding from one of the flanks is a matchless gem in its own right. Morando's original design was a little too modest and was altered in 1639-1651. The spectacular stairs in front of the building are a Baroque addition. Other monuments of note in Zamość include the Eastern-rite church of 1618-1631, the early 17th-century synagogue, and the building of the Zamość Academy. The Academy, established in 1595, made Zamość an important centre of intellectual life. It was intended by its founder to be a lay school for young noblemen, who were to be educated in a patriotic spirit.

1. Houses in the Market Square.
2. Zamość Town Hall.

➡ Tomaszów Lubelski – Baroque parish church built of larch wood; Bełżec – Nazi death camp, where thousands of Jews and Gypsies perished.

1. Arcades in the Market Square.
2. Decoration of the "Angel House".
3. Jan Zamoyski's epitaph in the collegiate church.

➡ Roztocze and the Puszcza Solska forest – a woodland landscape, wild horses and a cascade on the Tanew River; Klemensów – 18th-cent. palace and park.

KAZIMIERZ DOLNY

Kazimierz Dolny has been a merchant town for ages. The earliest sources that mention it date from the 12th century; it received its municipal charter in the 14th century from Kazimierz the Great. In the 16th century, the expansion of the Vistula trade brought vast revenues for the town's inhabitants.

Kazimierz still retained a medieval appearance at that time, but that was soon to change. It attained the peak of its development in the first half of the 17th century, when several dozen large granaries were in operation. Afterwards, gradual decline set in and the town became frozen in its enchanting form.

Amid loess hills and hollows, blooming orchards and fields, this town on the Vistula basks in its former glory. In the 19th century, Kazimierz Dolny became a well-known holiday destination and a site of plein-air sessions popular with artists. The town prides itself on its houses, especially those of the Przybyła family in the Market Square (St. Nicholas House and St. Christopher House; 1615) and the Celej House in Senatorska Street (1635). Their lavishly decorated façades are crowned with fancy parapets, which add about a third to the houses' overall height. The picturesque well in the centre of the Market Square dates from 1905, and the sizeable brick granaries at the edge of the town recall the times when grain was rafted down the Vistula. The stalls in the Market Square sell a local speciality - the pastry rooster – which is said to make an excellent ransom in the event of being accosted by the devil! The medieval castle ruins exude a romantic mood. According to legend, the castle was linked with the near-by Bochotnica Castle by an underground passage, supposedly built on the orders of King Kazimierz the Great, who used it for secret meetings with his beautiful Jewish mistress, Esther.

The hilltop parish Church of SS. John the Baptist and Bartholomew, originally Gothic, was remodelled in 1586–1589 and 1610–1613 in "Lublin Renaissance" style. Inside, the highlight is the 17th-century organ, the oldest completely preserved instrument of its kind in Poland.

1. A house in Kazimierz Dolny.
2. A riverside granary.
3. Windmill in Męćmierz on the outskirts of Kazimierz.

➡ Nałęczów – one of the most beautiful Polish spas; Czarnolas – manor house of the Renaissance poet Jan Kochanowski; the poet's tomb in Zwoleń.

AT THE FOOT OF THE CARPATHIANS

The Carpathians form Poland's natural border on the south, culminating in the Tatras, the only alpine fragment of the entire mountain chain, flanked by the undulating Beskidy and Gorce chains. The Tatra Mountains are divided into the High Tatras and West Tatras. While the former are extremely craggy and precipitous, the latter show a predominance of smoother forms, enriched by picturesque karst landscape. The numbers of visitors in the Highlands, enticed by the beautiful views, lively culture and "Zakopane-style" architecture, have been steadily on the increase since the 19th century. The Podhale region at the foot of the Tatras separates the latter from the Beskidy. A little further to the east extends a limestone belt comprising the extremely picturesque Pieniny Mountains, cut through by the wild Dunajec Gorge. Further away are the dome-shaped Beskidy peaks. The slopes are no longer very steep there, and the deep river valleys and ravines cut by smaller streams encompass remnants of the primeval Carpathian forest with age-old fir and beech. In the east, the spacious and almost uninhabited Bieszczady Mountains attract visitors with their majesty, mystery and peace. The unique and varied character of the Carpathian environment is attested to by the fact that as many as six national parks have been established in the region, in addition to the numerous reserves and other areas of protected landscape.

For centuries the Carpathians were a magnet for the adventurous: brave settlers, intrepid treasure-seekers, shepherds, outlaws and hermits. The region evolved a distinctive folklore in which Polish, Hungarian, Ruthenian and Walachian elements are amalgamated. Eastern-rite churches stood side by side with synagogues, monasteries arose next to fortified castles, and magnate palaces – amid shepherds' huts. In time, prosperous towns evolved on the major trade routes in the valleys, framed in scenic mountain settings.

1. A view of the Tatras from the Pieniny Mountains.
2. The Chapel at Jaszczurówka designed by Stanisław Witkiewicz.

THE TATRAS

The unique wildlife and landscape of the Tatra Mountains are protected by the Tatra National Park, which encompasses the Polish part of this sole alpine-type mountain range in the Carpathians. Geologically, the High Tatras are built mostly of crystalline rocks, and the West Tatras – of limestone, dolomite and metamorphic rocks. The highest peak on the Polish side is Mt. Rysy (2499 m above sea level). Rocky peaks, mountain tarns, broad valleys and steep gullies make up a world of exquisite, if harsh beauty. The scenery of the Tatras has always fired the imagination, giving rise to legends about knights sleeping in caves who would wake up at the sound of angel trumpets and hasten to the rescue of the imperilled native land. Some of the peaks have acquired a symbolic dimension, as in the case of Mt. Giewont, towering over Zakopane, with a cross at the summit looking onto the highlands. The major valleys in the Tatras run from south to north, the most important being the Chochołowska, Kościeliska, Mała Łąka, Bystra, Sucha Woda, Roztoka and Białka Valleys. The limestone parts of the range are the site of spectacular karst phenomena, and the Wielka Śnieżna cave ranks (at 776 metres) among the world's deepest. The Tatras abound in streams, cascading down the rocks. There are many protected plant species to be found, including the edelweiss, the crocus, varieties of the gentian, the smooth carline and the Arolla pine. Equally interesting is the animal world, with many rare mammals (chamois, brown bear, marmot, otter), birds (golden eagle, lesser spotted eagle, wall-creeper, black grouse) and insects (apollo butterfly – *Parnassius apollo*). However, their habitat is now endangered by the increased pressures of tourism, as ever-increasing numbers of people flock to see the inspirational and majestic beauty of the mountains. It is hard to believe that as late as in the 19th century large parts of the Tatras were dotted with mines and steelworks! Today, countless Tatra lovers ascend the rocky ridges every day, stop at the wooden hostels, drink the crystal-clear spring water. Seeing the Tatras provides an opportunity to ponder man's insignificance in the face of Nature.

1. Trail to the Szpiglasowa Pass.
2. Mount Giewont.

➡ Jurgów – old shepherds' huts; the atmospheric Białka Valley; Białka Tatrzańska – an old wooden church.

1. Lake Morskie Oko.
2. The Roztoka Valley.

➡ Gubałówka Hill above Zakopane, offering an excellent vantage point from which to admire the Tatras; Murzasichle – a small Highlander village with a breathtaking panorama of the mountains.

1. The Chochołowska Valley.
2. The "Five Polish Tarns" Valley.

➡ Ludźmierz – shrine of the Blessed Virgin Mary, the patroness of Podhale; extensive raised bogs in the vicinity.

ZAKOPANE AND CHOCHOŁÓW

The growing popularity of the Tatras stimulated an interest in the folklore and culture of the region's inhabitants. The "Zakopane style" was created at the turn of the 19th century by Stanisław Witkiewicz, who opposed the cosmopolitan vogue for "Swiss" architecture and made deliberate use of the structural patterns and architectural detail of the traditional Highland house, as these were thought to have retained traits of the "old Polish style". An important source of inspiration for Witkiewicz was the village of Chochołów, not far from Zakopane. Its old part, comprising several dozen extremely well preserved houses, is a unique "living cultural reserve". The village is densely built up, with the shorter sides of the houses facing the road. The houses are rich in carpentry detail, e.g., decorative door frames, timbering, ceiling rosettes and inscriptions. According to tradition, one of the Chochołów houses was built from a single trunk of an ancient fir tree. One of the houses accommodates a small local museum; another serves as a gallery of folk art.

Quite predictably, the Zakopane style is particularly well represented in the town of Zakopane itself – the bustling capital of the Polish Tatras. Its numerous historic buildings include the wooden parish church from 1847–1851, 19th-century Highlander houses and Zakopane-style villas built of timber, of which the oldest is called Koliba (1892) and the most beautiful – Dom Pod Jedlami ("Fir House"; 1897). This "Highland manor" was built on Koziniec hill for the Tatra explorer and conservationist Jan Gwalbert Pawlikowski. It is a timber cottage built on stone foundations, with a porch looking out on the Tatras. Witkiewicz designed not only the house itself, but also its furnishings, creating a unique and pure example of the Zakopane style. Also worth seeing are the chapel in Jaszczurówka (1908) and the Tatra Museum building (1913). The Zakopane style remains one of the best preserved and most frequently emulated trends in the architecture of the region.

1. Highlanders' house at Chochołów.
2. Koliba House interior.
3. Koliba House.

➡ Zakopane – historic cemetery at Pęksowy Brzyzek, ranking among the most important Polish necropolises; the old church and traditional houses next to the cemetery.

DĘBNO

Podhale is famous for its brick and timber architecture, representing both folk designs and various European styles. Among the most precious buildings are the wooden churches. The famous Archangel Michael Church in Dębno is one of the most beautiful and original architectural monuments in Poland. Like other 15th-century churches, it consists of a rectangular chancel and a broader, square nave, covered with a single-ridged roof. The tower with the characteristic overhanging upper part and the gallery surrounding the church exterior are later additions, probably dating from the early 17th century.

The church interior is in a class of its own, above all thanks to the beautifully preserved late 15th-century polychrome decoration, painted with the use of stencils. Ornamental motifs borrowed from Gothic traceries and tapestries prevail, with floral and, less often, figurative elements. One of these shows St. George slaying the dragon, and there are also depictions of hunters, deer and birds. The polychrome decoration covering the ceiling and chancel walls impresses with its vivid hues and somewhat resembles a colourful folk rug.

Particular mention should be made of the late Gothic high altar in the form of a triptych, with the Blessed Virgin Mary shown between St. Catherine and the patron of the church – the Archangel Michael – on the central panel, and other saints and Passion scenes painted against a golden background on the wings.

Also worthy of note are the Gothic sculptures (including a late 14th-century crucifix on the rood arch), a Gothic-style collator pew and an ancient tabernacle.

A fascinating discovery was made in the church loft twenty-odd years ago: a panel depicting SS. Agnes and Catherine. It dates from ca. 1300, which makes it the oldest surviving example of panel painting in Polish art.

1. The polychrome interior of church at Dębno (turn of the 15th cent.).
2. Church at Dębno Podhalańskie.

➡ Łopuszna – manor house of the Tetmajer family; Frydman – 16th-cent. fortified manor; old-time wine cellars.

SZALOWA

The simplicity and Gothic austerity of the Dębno church provide an interesting comparison with the buoyant Baroque forms at Szalowa. The latter church may seem distant from the one at Dębno both geographically (Szalowa lies near Gorlice, about 100 km to the east) and stylistically, but they are both exquisite examples of the use of timber, so typical of Polish architecture. The peculiarity of the Szalowa church consists in the mature imitation of monumental architecture, executed in timber. This must have been the work of an outstanding architect, though so far its authorship has eluded historians. As in Dębno, the church is dedicated to St. Michael the Archangel. Commissioned by Father Wojciech Stefanowski and the landowner Krzysztof Jordan, it was constructed in 1736–1756. It is an aisled basilica with a modest, twin-towered façade. Contrasting with the external appearance is the extremely rich and stylistically uniform interior, featuring a wealth of architectural forms, figurative murals and valuable furnishings. The high altar and six side altars are in late Baroque style with Rococo decorations from the mid-18th century. The sacristy holds a large collection of old liturgical items and valuable church vestments.

Dębno and Szalowa illustrate the immense architectural and cultural diversity of wooden churches in Poland, where timber has been used as a building material since pre-historic times. In the old days, it was used in the construction of all kinds of structures – dwellings, outbuildings, as well as sumptuous residences and houses of worship. Timber was abundant and easy to work, which explains its widespread use, leading to the evolution and diversification of regional features and patterns. Churches were always at the forefront of architecture. These masterpieces of carpentry would provide an appropriate setting for the development of religious and communal life. And church interiors have been veritable repositories of priceless works of art, from the Middle Ages to modern times.

1. Interior of the church at Szalowa.
2. Baroque portal in the chancel of the Szalowa church.

➜ Binarowa – magnificent wooden church, ca. 1500; Bobowa – historic 18th-cent. synagogue; Owczary – beautiful Uniate church from 1635.

THE PIENINY MOUNTAINS

Downstream from Dębno, the once narrow Dunajec river broadens into the expanse of an artificial lake, dividing the Pieniny from the Gorce range. At the foot of the Gorce is another fine monument of wooden architecture – St. Martin's Church at Grywałd, built in the latter half of the 15th century. Its nave is aisleless, and the tower has the characteristic overhang in its upper part.

On the opposite side of the Pieniny range stands Niedzica Castle, which for centuries constituted the northernmost point of the Kingdom of Hungary. The oldest part of the castle has been dated rather broadly to the late 13th century. Afterwards, the castle was gradually enlarged. In 1412, it was the scene of an important political event: Peter Schwarz of Lomnica, the treasurer to Sigismund of Luxembourg, King of Hungary, collected from King Władysław Jagiełło's envoys a loan of over 2 million Prague grossi, against the security of 16 towns of the Spisz region, ceded to Poland. In the 15th century, Niedzica Castle with the associated estate passed into the hands of the Zapolya family and then the Łaski family. In 1533–1535, the Zapolyas fought a private war against the Habsburgs and the castle became a hideout for robber-knights. In 1589, Olbracht Łaski sold Niedzica to the Horvath family, who modernised and enlarged the castle, which assumed a form close to its present appearance. The work was completed in 1601. The next owners were the Italian Joanelli family (ca. 1670), and towards the end of the 18th century, the decaying residence returned to the Horvaths. The last Niedzica lords (1858-1944) were the Salamon family. Gruesome legends are associated with the castle's dungeons, torture chambers and executions of highland robbers that used to take place there. There is also the story of a quipu supposedly found at the castle, identifying the place where an Inca treasure is said to be hidden! After the Second World War, the castle was thoroughly restored and opened for tourists. Unfortunately, the dam built in its immediate vicinity has somewhat marred the landscape, while the reservoir has flooded a once lovely fragment of the Dunajec valley.

1. Niedzica Castle.
2. Wooden church at Grywałd.
3. The Gorce Mountains.

➡ Szczawnica – a nicely situated spa with 19th-cent. guest houses; Kacwin village and its environs – traditional architecture of the Spisz region.

This is yet another corner of Poland that abounds in attractions – mineral waters, scenic views, vivid folklore and historic monuments recalling the times of the kings of Poland, Bohemia and Hungary. One of these is the ruins of a castle built in the 1280s by order of St. Kinga, who supposedly sought refuge in the mountains during a Tartar invasion.

The Pieniny legends also draw on the tradition of hermits, connected with the person of the future saint, Andrzej Świerad. The order of Poor Clares had a castle of its own built at today's Czorsztyn. However, this strategic stronghold, guarding the passage through the Dunajec valley, soon became Crown property.

In 1370, Czorsztyn was visited by Louis, King of Hungary and Poland, and in 1384, his daughter Jadwiga stopped there on her way to Cracow, where she was to ascend to the Polish throne. Her husband, King Władysław Jagiełło, was likewise a frequent visitor to Czorsztyn. According to legend, it was Poland's most valiant knight, Zawisza Czarny, who was the *starost* (Crown administrator) of Czorsztyn at the time. Yet another Polish monarch to visit the castle was Władysław of Varna, who sojourned there on his way to Hungary in 1440. Today, the castle has been reduced to a romantic-looking ruin, its outline reflected in the waters of the artificial lake.

The Pieniny Mountains offer numerous relatively easy hiking trails with beautiful views – for instance, to the peaks of Trzy Korony and Sokolica (can be combined into one excursion), or to the picturesque Homole ravine.

An attraction not to be missed is a raft trip down the Dunajec Gorge. The swift current, the limestone rocks towering above the wooden rafts, the sound of the flowing water and the tales of the raftsmen combine to form an unforgettable experience. It is not clear when the rafting tradition was initiated – legend associates its with Władysław Jagiełło. More tangible evidence is provided by a mural from 1589 at the church in Krościenko, depicting the patron saint of raftsmen. The rafting technique itself has not changed much since that date.

1. *Rafting in the Dunajec Gorge.*
2. *The Homole ravine.*
3. *A view from the summit of Mt. Sokolica.*

➡ Across the Gorce range – the enchanting town of Stary Sącz with the 13th-cent. convent of the Poor Clares.

KWIATOŃ AND ULUCZ

A mere 50 years ago, large parts of the Poprad valley were inhabited by a different Carpathian Highlander group – the Lemko. It was an area where Polish and Ruthenian culture coexisted and Roman Catholicism vied with the Orthodox and Uniate churches. The Lemko populated an area comprising the Beskid Niski and Beskid Sądecki Mountains, with an enclave at the foot of the Pieniny. Their origin has not been satisfactorily explained to date. They are believed to be the descendants of a tribe from Kievan Rus. Whatever their background, the Lemko ethnic group was broken up in 1947 as a result of "Operation Vistula", when they were deported – together with the Ukrainian minority – to northeastern and western Poland or to the Soviet Union. What they left behind were their eastern-rite churches. Timber architecture, which flourished in all the sub-Carpathian regions, evolved here in particularly decorative forms. From Roman Catholic churches, the Lemko adopted the tower with an overhang in its upper part, but added to it their own traditional elements, such as the broken roof and elaborate spires. St. Paraskevia's Uniate church in Kwiatoń was built in 1700, receiving a tower in 1743. Its layout is distinctly tripartite, with each of the sections built on a square plan. Preserved inside are polychrome decoration from 1811 and a complete 19th-century iconostasis. The church is surrounded with a fence, whose gate is likewise crowned with a bulbous spire.

The appearance of the Uniate Church of St. Nicholas at Ulucz is sterner. Built in 1510-1517 and partly remodelled in the 19th century, it is believed to be the oldest eastern-rite church in Poland. Originally, it was part of a fortified Basilian Friars' monastery. Like the church in Kwiatoń, it also employs a tripartite layout. Above the nave is an octagonal dome, while the overhanging eaves rest on the protruding tie-beams.

1. Uniate church at Kwiatoń.
2. Uniate church at Ulucz.

➤ Krynica – in its pre-war heyday, one of the most fashionable European spas; Muszyna – small-town architecture from times past.

BIECZ

While the ethnic composition of the sub-Carpathian villages was typically either predominantly Polish, or predominantly Ruthenian, the towns - and especially merchant towns - retained a multinational character. Biecz was no exception. The earliest reliable source document mentioning a settlement at this location dates from 1184, which suggests that a castellany existed there in the 12th century. However, the earliest mention of the Biecz castellans comes from 1243. In 1306, the Biecz *castrum* and its adjacent land was acquired by Bishop Jan Muskata, in exchange for the estate of Kamienica ceded to King Vaclav II. The Bishop did not keep his new possession for long, as it was soon captured by the Hungarians and than became part of the royal demesne. In the 15th-17th centuries, Biecz was an important centre of commerce and crafts, lying on the trade route linking Poland with Hungary. Until the Partitions of Poland, the town was the seat of the local starost (Crown administrator). A more sinister thread in the history of Biecz is connected with the school for executioners that existed there. The candidates for this profession could gain ample work experience, as Highland robbers were frequently put on trial before the local court. Biecz has retained its original urban plan, and numerous historic buildings have been preserved, including the richly furnished Corpus Christi parish church from the early 16th century. A double row of stone pillars supports the nave's ribbed net vault, which assumes a more elaborate cellular form above the chancel. The latter houses a monumental 16th-century high altar and late Renaissance painted stalls. Elsewhere, there is a surviving fragment of Biecz's 14th-16th century city walls, with a 16th-century fortified belfry. Baroque architecture is represented by church and monastery of the Reformati, while on the market square stands an impressive neo-Gothic town hall from 1830.

1

2

1. 17th-cent. music stand.
2. Stalls in the chancel of the Biecz parish church.

→ Gorlice – numerous cemeteries from 1915, a testimony to one of the largest battles of then First World War; the Magura National Park.

1. *View from Mt. Tarnica.*
2. *Eastern-rite church at Smolnik.*
3. *The Upper San valley in autumn.*

➡ Sanok – the castle, an open-air museum and a museum of icons; Haczów – the world's largest medieval wooden church.

THE BIESZCZADY MOUNTAINS

The Bieszczady are part of the Eastern Beskids, divided between Poland, Ukraine and Slovakia. Their Polish part comprises the parallel ridges of Wysoki Groń, Wołosań and Chryszczata, Durna, Połonina Wetlińska, Połonina Caryńska and Otryt. The highest peaks are: Tarnica (1346 m above sea level), Halicz (1333 m) and Bukowe Berdo (1312 m). Some of the uncommon natural features of this mountain range include lakes formed by landslides and raised bogs in the Upper San valley. The greater part of the Polish Bieszczady is encircled by the "Bieszczady Circuit" – a scenic route that begins and ends in the town of Lesko. The highest areas of the mountains are situated within the Bieszczady National Park, established in order to protect the wildlife and landscape of the East Carpathians. Vegetation zones in the Bieszczady follow a different vertical distribution pattern than in other mountain ranges. Above the lower forest zone, which occupies 80% of the National Park's area, there is a narrow belt of green alder, rowan and dwarf beech, above which there is no upper forest zone (commonly found elsewhere). Instead, there are extensive mountain meadows. The fauna of the Bieszczady includes the bear, deer, wolf, lynx, wildcat and also the European bison, introduced after the war. There are also rare species of bird, such as the Ural owl, Alpine accentor, golden eagle or three-toed woodpecker – and the extremely rare Aesculapian snake. Apart from the National Park, there are many reserves in the Bieszczady, including a lynx reserve on the slopes of Mt. Wielka Rawka, the Wołosate peat bog, and the beech-and-sycamore Wetlina forest. The Bieszczady valleys used to be densely populated. However, the indigenous population, consisting of the Lemko and, occasionally, Boyko ethnic groups, was deported after 1945, in the aftermath of the clashes with the underground Ukrainian Insurrectionary Army (UPA). All that is left today are some historic eastern-rite churches and a few cottages that have been moved to the open-air museum in Sanok. Gone are the old villages, and the only reminders of the area's one-time inhabitants are an occasional neglected orchard, a tilted roadside cross or a patch overgrown with nettle.

1. *Połonina Wetlińska and Połonina Caryńska peaks.*
2. *The Wołosate peat bog.*
3. *Charcoal production.*

➡ Kalwaria Pacławska – a shrine founded by the Fredro family; Posada Rybotycka – a fortified Uniate church from the 16th cent.

TARNÓW

The early history of Tarnów is intertwined with that of the powerful Lelewita family from Małopolska, whose descendants assumed in time the name of Tarnowski. For centuries, Tarnów remained a private town, but this changed in 1787, when its last owner, Prince Eustachy Sanguszko, renounced his authority over it. Tarnów abounds in cultural relics. Embedded in the framework of the preserved medieval plan are architectural monuments from many epochs. One of the most valuable of these is the Gothic-Renaissance town hall with a parapet. Equally significant is the old collegiate church (now a cathedral), with a series of Tarnowski-family tombs and the monumental Ostrowski mausoleum. The stone monuments set into the walls represent various phases of Renaissance, Mannerist and Baroque art. Old residential housing in Tarnów illustrates the transformation of the burgher house from the 16th to the 20th century, and the partly preserved ring of walls indicates that the town was well protected. Also within the town perimeter are two timber churches, from the 15th and 16th century; a little further away are the ruins of the Tarnowski Castle on Góra Św. Marcina ("St. Martin's Hill") and the late 18th-century Sanguszko Palace complex in the district of Gumniska. Another place of historical interest is the tomb of General Józef Bem, a hero of Poland and Hungary, in the city park.

Of the city's museums, especially worth seeing are the Cathedral Treasury (the exhibits include priceless liturgical items from the Benedictine abbey at Tyniec) and the Diocesan Museum (unique medieval and Renaissance religious art). The highlights of the collection are the wings of a triptych from Kasina Wielka with standing figures of saints, a triptych from Gosprzydowa, a painting from Szczepanów (ca. 1470) representing St. Stanisław, the famous Deposition of Christ from the Chomranice church, and a lyrical image of the Virgin with a carnation from the church on St. Martin's Hill near Tarnów. There is also an interesting collection of liturgical vestments from the Middle Ages and modern times.

1. Tarnów town hall.
2. The tomb of Barbara Tarnowska née Tęczyńska in Tarnów Cathedral.

➜ Dębno – a 15th century castellan's seat where jousting tournaments are reenacted today; Rożnów Reservoir – a water sports centre.

LEŻAJSK

Leżajsk received its charter in 1397, but at that time it was situated in a different place, corresponding to the present village of Stara Wieś. Frequent Tartar raids caused the town to be moved to its present, more secure location in 1524. Those were by no means peaceful times. Apart from Swedish, Tartar and Russian invaders, local magnates could be equally oppressive. In 1607-1610 the *starost* (Crown administrator) of Leżajsk, Łukasz Opaliński, waged a bloody, private war against his neighbour, Stanisław Stadnicki, in which thousands of soldiers were involved. In 1609, Stadnicki's mercenaries captured and looted Leżajsk.

The historical layout of the town from its most prosperous epoch has been preserved. Other monuments of the past include the 17th-century Bernardine monastery complex, the 17th century Holy Trinity Church, an 18th-century palace complex and a Uniate church from the 19th century.

The Bernardine monastery was built as a stronghold. The design of its walls and towers is attributed to Krzysztof Mieroszewski. At the heart of the monastery is the Church of the Annunciation (1618––1628), which boasts splendid polychrome interior decoration, sculpture and furnishings. The tabernacle at the high altar is the work of the Lvov sculptor A. Osiński. However, the most important historical monument is the famous Leżajsk organ from the late 18th century, equipped with 74 registers and 5894 pipes. Pilgrims head for the Chapel of the Blessed Virgin Mary to see the miraculous painting of St. Mary, venerated since 1634. Another image of the Virgin, displayed in the sacristy, is attributed to Albrecht Dürer. The monastery museum possesses a rich and diverse collection of religious art and incunabula.

In the 18th century, the town became a centre of Hasidism. The grave of zaddick Elimelech (d. 1787), better known as Majlech of Leżajsk, at the Jewish cemetery is visited by Jews from all over the world.

1. Bernardine church and monastery in Leżajsk.
2. The Leżajsk organ.
3. Aisle in Leżajsk church.

➡ Sieniawa – the former mansion of the Sieniawski family; Jarosław – a beautiful old town with many interesting buildings and a fortified Benedictine abbey.

BARANÓW

Baranów Sandomierski lies on the Vistula, in the Tarnobrzeg lowlands. Its chief tourist attraction is the Leszczyński Castle, one of the most beautiful Mannerist buildings in Poland. It superseded an earlier structure, built by Jakub of the Grzymała clan, a Crown official in Sandomierz. In 1569, Palatine Rafał Leszczyński embarked on the construction of what is now the castle's east wing. The main part of the work was carried out in 1591–1606, under the supervision of Santi Gucci. Baranów was owned at that time by Andrzej Leszczyński, Palatine of Brześć and Kujawy. The complex consists of a residential section and fortifications, the castle itself having been built on a rectangular plan with four cylindrical corner towers and an arcaded inner courtyard. The arcades are attributed to Santi Gucci's workshop, which the artist established in Pińczów, attracted by the proximity of a quarry. The workshop produced what we would call today "prefabricated" elements of masonry and sculpture, which would sometimes be transported to fairly distant "construction sites". Baranów bears witness to the extremely strong impact of the Wawel arcaded courtyard in Cracow. The arcades at Baranów, both tiers of which have Ionic columns (Gucci's favourite) display elegance and an eye for detail. The building became crowned with fancy gables and parapets. By order of Józef Karol Lubomirski, the residence was enlarged to the design of Tylman van Gameren (ca. 1695). The western wing of the castle was remodelled, and the interior layout and decoration were modernised. Care was also taken of the fortification system. Like many other residences, Baranów was devastated after the war, but over the years, painstaking conservation work has restored it to its former state. Today, it houses a castle museum and an exhibition devoted to the archaeology and geology of the surrounding region, which is rich in sulphur deposits. In the 17th century, Baranów Sandomierski was a centre of Calvinism. The Leszczyńskis established a printing press there and published dissident writings.

1. *Arcaded courtyard of the castle at Baranów Sandomierski.*
2. *Baranów Castle.*

➡ Sandomierz Forest with many nature reserves; old buildings at Kolbuszowa – the synagogue, housing a collection of Kolbuszowa furniture.

Krasiczyn

The attraction of Krasiczyn is the late Renaissance mansion. Initially, there was only a small castle at this site, the property of Jakub of Siecin. His modest residence was enlarged towards the end of the 16th century by Stanisław Sieciński, who changed his name to Krasicki upon founding the town of Krasiczyn.

Palatine Marcin Krasicki, who had inherited the castle, embarked on major remodelling at the end of the 16th century, giving the castle the form of a fortress built on the plan of an irregular quadrangle with cylindrical corner towers and a gate-tower with a foregate. The work proceeded in stages from 1598 to 1633. It is probably to the architect Galeazzo Appiani that the castle owes its final shape.

In accordance with the pious spirit of the time and the nobility's penchant for hierarchies, the four towers received appropriate names: Divine, Papal, Royal and Noblemen's. Predictably, the most conspicuous is the Divine Tower, crowned with a dome and decorated with large sgraffiti on the walls. Two other towers culminate in parapets, while the Royal tower has a wreath of decorative turrets around the top, which make it look like a crown. The arcades running around the courtyard at ground-floor level give the residence the appearance of a palace. Large sections of the walls, both in the courtyard and outside, have sgraffito decoration. On the courtyard-facing parapet of the east wing, these take the form of medallions with the heads of Roman emperors and Polish kings; on the outer wall, there are hunting scenes.

Unfortunately, nothing has been preserved of the old furnishings. The castle burnt down in 1852 and the effects of the reconstruction, undertaken soon afterwards, were erased during the First World War. In 1939, the magnificent decoration of the chapel was destroyed by the Red Army. The castle was surrounded by a beautiful park. Today, thanks to the conservators' efforts, Krasiczyn is being restored to its former awe-inspiring splendour.

1. Krasiczyn Castle.
2. Courtyard of the castle.

➡ Przemyśl – an old town spread across hills, the site of many historic buildings; 19th-cent. forts around Przemyśl, which made up one of the largest fortresses in Europe at the time.

1. The Potocki Palace at Łańcut.
2. Façade facing the garden.
3. The Green Drawing Room.

➡ Przeworsk – monastery complex with the late Gothic Church of the Holy Ghost; Bernardine Monastery; "Pastewnik" – a historic inn, now a museum.

ŁAŃCUT

The "Golden Liberty" so beloved of the nobility had a peculiar tendency to degenerate into insubordination or downright anarchy. When it comes to notoriety, no one could outdo Stanisław Stadnicki (1551?–1610), the lord at Łańcut, whose unparalleled cruelty earned him the nickname of "The Łańcut Devil". His fortified castle passed into the hands of Stanisław Lubomirski, who transformed it in the years 1629–1641 into a beautiful early Baroque *palazzo in fortezza*. The work was probably supervised by Matteo Trapola. The new structure was surrounded with pentagonal fortifications complete with bastions and deep moats, while the once-fortified corner towers of the castle were altered to serve a decorative purpose. Towards the end of the 17th century, Sebastian Lubomirski commissioned Tylman van Gameren to carry out construction work at Łańcut, but his contribution was limited to modernisation of the fortifications. Remodelling went on at Łańcut for many more years, supervised, among others, by Szymon Bogumił Zug and Jan Chrystian Kamsetzer. Today's appearance of the palace is due to Christian Piotr Aigner (end of the 18th century) and to the eclectic transformations effected in the years 1889–1912. In 1816, the palace passed to the Potockis. The interiors (housing an enormous collection of art, weapons and artistic handicraft, as well as an excellent library), untouched by wartime destruction, attract numerous visitors. However, the most precious items from the Lubomirski and Potocki collection are missing. Towards the end of the Second World War, the last owner, Alfred Potocki, fled before the advancing Red Army, taking abroad with him 11 railway cars filled with family movables. Visitors to Łańcut can see the ballroom, theatre, a suite of reception rooms and the living quarters, decorated in a variety of styles, from Rococo to Biedermeier and Art Nouveau. The interiors also provide an appropriate setting for prestigious music festivals, political conferences and summits. Surrounding the palace is a spacious landscaped park, and the old coach-house is now a museum of carriages and gear, one of the largest such collections in Europe. The town of Łańcut itself boasts a well-preserved historical plan and a Baroque synagogue of 1761.

1. Łańcut coach-house.
2. Inside the palace.
3. The palace park.

➡ Blizne – 16th-cent. wooden church and 18th-cent. vicarage buildings; Odrzykoń – ruins of the 14th century castle.

S I L E S I A

Silesia owes its name to the Ślężanie tribe (7th-9th centuries), but the history of settlement in this land is far older. The division into Lower and Upper Silesia originates from 1177, when Prince Bolesław the Tall ceded the province of Racibórz to his brother, Mieszko the Bandylegged. Afterwards, each of the two provinces followed its own route – politically, ethnically and culturally – although their subsequent history would often intertwine. Lower Silesia became an enchanting land of fields and forests, full of relics of the past immersed in legend. From the 13th century onwards, the former Piast principalities underwent gradual Germanisation, largely under the influence of German settlers, mostly from Franconia. The princes themselves, beginning with Bolesław the Bald, became Germanised, too. Meanwhile, Upper Silesia developed a strong economy, based on mining, metallurgy and heavy industry. The Polish population prevailed in its ethnic composition until the 18th century, when the province came under Prussian rule. In the 19th century, a Polish national consciousness awoke in Upper Silesia. At the Peace Conference in Paris (1918–1919), when Poland advanced claims for Upper Silesia and the Opole region, a Polish-German conflict ensued, culminating in three Silesian Uprisings, as a result of which part of Upper Silesia was incorporated into Poland. The rights of the German minority in those territories were guaranteed and the province was granted autonomy. The Second World War changed the situation completely. By decision of the Big Four, Silesian Germans were deported to Germany, and the province became re-settled with Poles evicted from the former Polish borderlands in the east, which now had fallen prey to Stalin. Geographically, Silesia comprises varied landscapes – from the peaks of the Sudetes, through the extensive Silesian Lowlands cut by the valleys of the Odra and its tributaries, to the Silesian Uplands culminating in St. Anne's Hill. In the Opole Plain, there survive fragments of the primeval Silesian Forest.

1. *Ruins of Chojnik Castle in the Karkonosze Mountains.*
2. *"Wang" – a Scandinavian wooden church brought over to Karpacz.*

KSIĄŻ

In terms of cubic capacity (ca. 160,000 m³), Książ is one of the largest historic buildings in Poland. The castle is situated on a high, promontory-type hill at a bend of the Pełczyca River in the picturesque Książ Protected Landscape Area. Raised towards the end of the 13th century by Prince Bolko I of Świdnica and Jawor, it remained for decades the seat of the Silesian princes. This fortified structure, known as Fürstenstein, was built on an irregular plan, with a quadrangular tower guarding the entrance.

The Gothic-Renaissance castle was built in 1548–1555 for the wealthy Hochberg family, who lived there from 1509 until the Second World War. This new castle was in turn remodelled and enlarged in 1718–1734 with an imposing late Baroque corpus designed by the architect Felix Anton Hammerschmidt, whose collaborators included the painter F.A. Scheffler and the sculptor J.G. Schenk. Their work transformed the castle into a residence with splendid interiors (for instance, the Maximilian Hall). In the 19th century, the castle's owners went up in the world. In 1848, the Hochbergs became connected through marriage with the von Pless family from Pszczyna in Upper Silesia, and in 1855 had a ducal title conferred upon them. In 1855, remodelling of the lower castle and the castle gardens was commenced; the structure known as the "lower gate" was converted into the castle library. In 1908–1923, a monumental, neo-Renaissance suite, with two corner towers, was built on the initiative of Hans Heinrich XV. At the same time, a neo-Renaissance crowning was added to the 48-metre high main tower.

The castle suffered the disastrous effects of a Nazi plan to convert it into a residence for Hitler. Although this idea was never put into practice, some of the interiors were destroyed during the preparatory work. Tunnels were dug underneath the castle by prisoners from a subsidiary of the Gross-Rosen concentration camp. Further devastation of the castle complex occurred after the war, but it has since been painstakingly restored.

1. *Drawing room in the castle.*
2. *General view of the eclectic Książ Castle.*

➡ Świdnica – old market square with the town hall and half-timbered Church of Peace; Jawor – Church of Peace; Sobótka Hill – a pagan ritual site of the Ślężanie tribe.

THE KARKONOSZE MOUNTAINS

The Sudetes are an old mountain group, the product of repeated folding, comprising a number of ranges largely differing in landscape. Their westernmost part, called the Izerskie Mountains, is separated from the Karkonosze range by the Szklarska Pass. The Karkonosze are crowned by Mt. Śnieżka (1602 m above sea level), the highest peak in the Sudetes. Its characteristic coneshaped summit rising some 200 metres above the flat ridge commands a magnificent view which has attracted visitors for centuries. Nowadays, Mt. Śnieżka is among the most frequently climbed peaks in Poland. On the top stand a 17th-century chapel, a weather station and a mountain hostel.

A pronounced feature of the Karkonosze landscape is the presence of cirques with lakes at their floors, attesting to the one-time glaciation of the range. Weathering has given rise to unusual rock formations with fancy names, such as "Horse Heads", "Pilgrims", "Sunflower" or "Three Towers" (in a similar spirit, the German name of the range, Riesengebirge, stands for "Mountains of the Giants"). These have given rise to innumerable legends, usually of a rather murky kind. Five vegetation zones can be distinguished in the Karkonosze, the habitat of many rare plant and animal species. This unique environment is protected by the Karkonosze National Park.

Many popular holiday resorts are situated at the foot of the Karkonosze, such as Karpacz, Bierutowice, Szklarska Poręba and Kowary. The trail from Karpacz to Mt. Śnieżka passes a rare and unusual sight – a small wooden church named "Wang", built in the 13th century in southern Norway. It was acquired in 1841 by the Prussian King Frederick William IV, and a year later the timbers covered with runic inscriptions were reassembled in Lower Silesia.

The Jelenia Góra Basin at the foot of the mountains used to be guarded by Chojnik Castle, once the property of the Schaffgotsch family. The oldest mountain range of the Sudetes, the Sowie ("Owl") Mountains, abuts on the Bardzkie and Złote mountain ridges. The entire area has a good tourist infrastructure; there are also several attractive spas, some of which have been frequented by patients for centuries.

1. The Karkonosze National Park.
2. Winter in the Karkonosze.
3. Wielki Staw tarn.

➡ Gryfów, Lwówek Śląski, Głogów, Legnica – typical Lower Silesian towns, with market squares and interesting churches.

THE STOŁOWE MOUNTAINS

The largest depression in the Sudety region is the Kłodzko Basin, flanked by the picturesque Góry Stołowe (or "Table Mountain") range. This is the only instance of tableland in Poland, built of calcareous sandstone and marl, which produces spectacular rock forms, as in the case of the highest point of this mountain group – Mt. Wielki Szczeliniec (919 m above sea level). Weathering processes have transformed the rock into a veritable maze of passages, fissures and bizarre shapes. Another interesting place in the Stołowe Mountain National Park is the Błędne Skały ("Labyrinthine Rocks") reserve.

Behind the Stołowe Mountains lies the Kłodzko Basin, which cradles the valleys of the Nysa Kłodzka and its tributaries. The town of Kłodzko existed already in the 10th century as a fortified settlement. It received its charter in the 13th century, and from the mid-18th century was the capital of a county under Bohemian rule. Situated on a strategically important trade route, Kłodzko was a large centre of commerce and crafts, operating its own mint and employing mercenary soldiers.

In the 14th century, part of *St. Florian's Psalter*, one of the oldest texts in Polish literature, was composed at the Canons Regular monastery in Kłodzko. The town's historic monuments include a late Gothic basilica from the 15th-16th centuries, a Baroque Jesuit college, the formerly Franciscan Church of the Blessed Virgin Mary with a monastery (17th-18th centuries), fragments of medieval city walls, a Gothic bridge and a 17th-century fortress. No one ever tried to capture the fortress, towering formidably above the town, and it thus served as a prison. Today, it is open to visitors, as is Srebrna Góra some distance away, an 18th-century fortress with 12-metre thick brick walls.

Another natural wonder worth visiting in the Eastern Sudetes is the Jaskinia Niedźwiedzia ("Bear's Cave") in the Śnieżnik massif – one of the most spectacular caves in Poland. The overall length of its passages is close to 3,000 metres, and the cave is protected as a geological reserve.

1. *The Stołowe Mountains.*
2. *The rocks of Mały Szczeliniec.*
3. *Stalactites in the "Bear's Cave".*

→ Złoty Stok – a 15th-century gold mine; Bardo – a historic town with a Baroque basilica; Czermna – a chapel decorated with 3,000 skulls.

WROCŁAW

The capital of Lower Silesia, Wrocław, belonged for many centuries to the most affluent and beautiful towns of Central Europe. Initially a stronghold of the Ślężanie tribe, it had evolved by the late 10th century into a large, fortified settlement occupying the island of Ostrów Tumski on the Odra river, which stood guard – alongside Legnica and Głogów – over the western flank of the early Piast state ruled by Prince Mieszko I. The development of Wrocław gained speed in the 12th century, when Piotr Włostowic founded the monasteries of the Benedictines at Ołbin (ca. 1120–1128) and the Augustinians at Piasek (ca. 1148). Towards the end of the 13th century, construction began of the Holy Cross Church (completed in 1350), one of the most precious monuments of Gothic architecture in Poland.

As early as the turn of the 12th century, the town spread onto the left bank of the Odra, where a market square came into being, together with stalls and merchants' houses. After the destruction wreaked by the Tartar invasion of 1241, the town's charter was renewed in the following year. Around 1263, a new town was established, now the district of Nowe Miasto. Wrocław was an expanding centre of commerce, crafts and culture. It maintained links with Flanders, France, Italy, and even Ireland, and was engaged in trade with Ruthenia, Byzantium and towns on the Rhine.

The Town Hall, now the seat of the Historical Museum of Wrocław, has always been the pride and joy of the city's inhabitants. Erected in the latter half of the 13th century, it was totally remodelled in late Gothic style in 1471–1504, when it received original and refined sculptural decoration. The open-air cafés that abound in the beautifully restored Old Town provide an excellent vantage point from which to admire the Town Hall, which also has a popular beer tavern – Piwnica Świdnicka – in its cellars from the 13th century. Under Henryk the Bearded (1202–1238) and his son, Henry the Pious (1238–1241), Wrocław maintained its position of the strongest town in the region, mainly because of the numerous privileges it received. As quickly as it was getting rich, Wrocław was becoming Germanised, mostly through the influx of settlers during the rule of Henryk the Bearded and Henryk Probus (ca. 1258–1290).

1. *The Aula Leopoldina at Wrocław University.*
2. *The Town Hall in Wrocław's Main Market Square.*

➡ The Ossolineum Library on Szewska street, housing one of the most important collections of old books and manuscripts in Poland.

After the death of Prince Henryk VI of the Piast dynasty (1335), the town, together with the entire principality of Wrocław, found itself in the orbit of Bohemian influence, and in the 16th century came under Habsburg rule.

Despite the destruction caused by the Thirty Years' War, culture and education thrived in Wrocław. In 1702, a Jesuit academy was established, which would be transformed into a university in 1811. The immense college building was just a fragment of the complex that the Jesuits planned to build on the Odra. The scale of their project is best illustrated by the splendour of the University's main assembly hall – the Aula Leopoldina, with decorations by Johann Albrecht Siegwitz, Franz Joseph Mangold, and Johann Christoph Handke. Its sumptuous, Baroque interior is adorned with sculptures, stuccoes and trompe l'oeil murals.

In 1741, Wrocław was captured by the Prussians. Despite an intense campaign of Germanisation, the Polish language was often heard in the town until the mid-19th century. In the 1930s, Wrocław had a population of about 630,000 and was the eighth largest town in Germany. In 1945, it was the scene of bitter fighting between German and Soviet troops, which reduced the town to rubble. Many relics of the past have now been reconstructed.

With a view to recreating the magnificent traditions of Wrocław, several Polish academic and cultural institutions, including the Ossolineum Library were relocated there from Lvov. Nowadays, Wrocław has nine institutions of higher education and nine major museums, the most frequently visited of which is the National Museum, specialising in Silesian guild art and Polish painting. Displayed in a nearby rotunda is the largest Polish canvas in existence – *The Panorama of Racławice Battlefield* by Wojciech Kossak and Jan Styka. It, too, was brought over from Lvov.

Wrocław's historic buildings include Gothic and Baroque churches, as well as interesting housing from the 19th and early 20th centuries. In the district of Piasek, there is a Augustinian monastery with a Gothic hall church (ca. 1334–1375) that survived the war. Set amongst the houses and palaces from the 14th-19th centuries are many churches, including the 15th-century Gothic Church of St. Mary Magdalene, incorporating a Romanesque portal from the former Ołbin Abbey.

1. St. Martin, National Museum in Wrocław.
2. Crown from a treasure trove discovered at Środa Śląska.

➡ The People's Hall (formerly Centennial Hall), built in 1913 to Max Berg's design to commemorate the 100th anniversary of the Battle of Leipzig – 42 metres high and 130 metres wide.

WROCŁAW

In the year 1000, a bishopric was established in Wrocław, which until 1821 was subordinated to the metropolitan see in Gniezno. The town's oldest buildings are the dominant accent of the townscape of Ostrów Tumski island, which includes a Gothic cathedral with Romanesque elements from 1149. In those early days, the religious edifices and the prince's residence on the island made up the largest architectural complex of Romanesque Poland. The cathedral's chancel was built in 1244–1272, while its basilican corpus dates from 1302–1376. On the west, the cathedral terminates in a twin-towered façade, and on the east is the exquisite Chapel of St. Mary, flanked by two Baroque chapels. The one to the south, dedicated to St. Elizabeth, is an outstanding achievement of Baroque art. It was erected and decorated in 1680–1686 by Italian artists commissioned by Cardinal Frederick of Hesse. The other chapel, called the Elector's Chapel to commemorate its founder, Bishop Franz Ludwig von Neuenburg, was built in 1715–1724 to the design of the Viennese architect Johann Bernard Fischer von Erlach. The cathedral, dedicated to St. John the Baptist, the patron saint of the diocese, was rebuilt after the fire of 1945 and restored to its former Gothic appearance.

The high altar contains a 16th-century triptych of the Dormition of the Blessed Virgin Mary. It was brought from Lubin and is believed to have come from the workshop of Veit Stoss. Not far from the cathedral is the Bishops' Palace (1791), incorporating architectural details dating from the 12th century, as well as canons' houses and parish offices.

The rich and interesting collection of the Archdiocesan Museum, also located on Ostrów Tumski, includes many excellent works of art and craft. One of the highlights is the oldest bell in Poland, over seven centuries old. Yet another historic monument on the island is the collegiate Holy Cross Church – a two-level Gothic hall from the 13th-14th centuries. Next to the Tumski Bridge stands the small Church of SS. Peter and Paul, with a vault supported on a single pillar. Also worth visiting is the nearby 12th-century Church of St. Martin.

1. The Cathedral on Ostrów Tumski island.
2. Romanesque portal from the former Ołbin Abbey.

➡ Trzebnica – a Cistercian nuns' abbey with the St. Jadwiga of Silesia Chapel; Milicz ponds – a large bird sanctuary; Antonin – wooden hunting lodge of the Radziwiłł family.

1. *Interior of St. John the Baptist's Church.*
2. *Entrance to the St. Elizabeth Chapel.*

➡ Oleśnica – ducal town with a castle and city walls; Lubiąż – huge Baroque post-Cistercian monastery (223-metre long façade).

WAMBIERZYCE AND OPOLE

Lower Silesia is a land where, despite shifting political boundaries and population migrations, common cultural roots have been preserved. One instance is the shrine at Wambierzyce – a traditional pilgrimage site of the Czechs, situated in Poland. It occupies a depression between the Stołowe Mountains and the Kamienne Mountains to the south. The locals derive their livelihood from pilgrims and tourists who come to see the basilica and calvary. The layout of Wambierzyce reflects that of Jerusalem in the times of Christ. The shrine owes its existence to a small, late 14th-century figure of the Madonna and Child, which became an object of religious cult. It was for the pilgrims that the church was raised at the turn of the 17th century. It is built on an octagonal plan inscribed in a complex of auxiliary buildings, and is preceded by a magnificent flight of steps (1715–1720). The tiny market square at Wambierzyce can be approached through one of the 12 gates – reminiscent of Jerusalem. Another attraction, in nearby Czermna, is an old Nativity crèche containing 800 figures, set in motion by a special mechanism.

The ancient Piast settlement of Opole is today the capital of a region where the cultural revival of the German minority in Silesia takes its fullest form. Bilingual schools and monuments are springing up everywhere. The character of the region is changing, or, to put it differently, the multiethnic fabric of Central Europe, destroyed by totalitarianism, is now being recreated. Opole's historical tradition is epitomised by the Franciscan Church, which for centuries served as the necropolis for the Opole line of the Piast dynasty. These former rulers rest in peace under the stellar vault of the Gothic St. Anne's Chapel. Nearby stands the tower of the Piast castle, as does the Holy Cross Church, built in the 13th/14th centuries. When the Opole line of the Piasts expired in 1532, the town passed into the hands of the Hohenzollerns and then the Habsburgs; in 1645–1665 it was pledged to Poland, and in 1742 came under Prussian rule. Today, it is wellknown as the venue of an annual song festival.

1. Tombs of the Piast princes of Opole in the Franciscan Church of the Holy Trinity.
2. Shrine of the Blessed Virgin Mary at Wambierzyce.

➤ Bystrzyca Kłodzka – Water Tower (16th cent.); Duszniki – market square; Museum of the Paper Industry; whale-shaped Baroque pulpit in the parish church.

BRZEG

The earliest records mentioning Brzeg date from the 11th century. Upon the division of the Principality of Wrocław in 1311, it was made the capital of the Principality of Legnica and Brzeg, which became a Bohemian fief in 1329. The last of the Legnica-Brzeg Piasts, Prince Georg-Wilhelm, died in 1675. His death signalled the end of prosperity for this once affluent town, which thereafter came under direct Habsburg rule. The most valuable historic monument in Brzeg is the Piast Castle with a 14th-century Gothic chapel and an arcaded courtyard. A princely court in Brzeg was mentioned as early as 1235, and a castle was probably built there around 1300. It was next enlarged (possibly before 1342) by Prince Bolesław III, who resided in Brzeg. The chapel – initially a collegiate church – was constructed in 1368–1371. In 1541, Prince Frederick II commenced the remodelling of the residence as a Renaissance palace. This task was entrusted to the brothers Francesco and Giacomo Parr, who hired a part-Italian and part-Silesian team of bricklayers, stonemasons and sculptors. After Frederick's death in 1547, the work was continued by his son Georg II. Unfortunately, following the Battle of Małujowice during the War of Austrian Succession in 1741, the castle came under Prussian fire and was not fully restored until the 1990s.

The most impressive part of the castle is the gate, whose façade is decorated with figurative sculptures from 1556–1560 – a masterpiece of the Silesian Renaissance. This was the work of the Silesian sculptors Andreas Walther, Kaspar Kuhne and Jacob Werter. Above the doorway are two life-size statues of the founder and his wife Barbara, accompanied by footmen holding immense escutcheons. Further up still is the family tree of Prince Georg and numerous scenes glorifying his deeds. Elsewhere in Opole there is also a Renaissance town hall from 1570–1577, a Gothic parish church from the turn of the 14th century, and a Baroque Jesuit church from 1734–1739.

1. "Ancestors' Gallery" on the gate-tower façade.
2. Gate-tower façade and chapel at the Silesian Piast Castle.

➨ Paczków – well-preserved 14th-cent. city walls; Nysa – the Old Town with the 15th-cent. Gothic cathedral.

Krzeszów

Lower Silesia boasts one of the largest Baroque churches in Poland, situated in the village of Krzeszów, which was linked from the Middle Ages with the Cistercian abbey founded in 1292 by Prince Bolko the Stern of Świdnica. The abbey, which suffered major damage during the Hussite wars and the Thirty Years' War, was restored in the 18th century.

The Abbey Church of St. Mary is a monument of exceptional rank. Built in 1728–1735, it is decorated with murals by J.W. Neunhertz from 1733–1735 and sculptures by the Bohemian masters A. Dorasil and Ferdinand Maximilian Brokof (before 1775). Strangely, the designer of this imposing church is not known, although the work was certainly supervised by Anton Joseph Jentsch, a native Silesian from Kamienna Góra. (The hypothetical attribution of the church to Kilian Ignatz Dientzenhofer has been abandoned.) In terms of its proportions, the avoidance of straight lines and architectural mastery, the edifice is reminiscent of the Baroque, formerly Benedictine Church of St. Jadwiga at Legnickie Pole – another first-rank monument.

Abutting on the Krzeszów church is the Świdnica Piast Mausoleum from 1735–1747, with the 14th-century Gothic tombs of Princes Bolko I and Bolko II. The Mausoleum consists of two connected chapels. Both the medieval and modern tombs seem lost in the profusion of sculpture and trompe l'oeil painting.

The abbey church is a galleried hall with a spacious transept and twin-towered façade. Seen from a distance, the church presents a charming silhouette with its two graceful towers rising above fields and hills. Upon closer view, one is immediately struck by the harmonious jux-taposition of the façade's architectural and sculptural elements. The nearby parish Church of St. Joseph has beautiful Baroque murals from 1695 by Michael Leopold Willman.

1. *The abbey church at Krzeszów.*
2. *Inside the nave.*
3. *Tomb of Prince Bolko II of Świdnica.*

➜ The Sowie Mountains (Osówka and Walim) – secret underground shelters and galleries cut in the rock by prisoners; Zagórz – one of the most beautiful Silesian castles.

WIELKOPOLSKA AND KUJAWY

Numerous river valleys and lakes lend variety to the flat, occasionally gently rolling landscape of Wielkopolska and Kujawy. Tree-lined alleys lead to old mansions and palaces surrounded with lush, green parks. Nowhere in Poland has agriculture developed so well, and this is often attributed to the diligence and famously innovative spirit of the region's inhabitants.

Wielkopolska was the historic centre of Poland. In the 10th century, Ziemomysł, the ruler of the Polanie tribe, united his territories into a fully-fledged state. It was from Wielkopolska that Ziemomysł's successor, Prince Mieszko I, began the Christianisation of Poland. However, a Bohemian invasion launched after the death of Mieszko II less than a hundred years later wreaked widescale destruction, inducing Prince Kazimierz the Restorer to move the capital to Cracow. When, in his testament of 1138, King Bolesław the Wry-mouthed divided the state among his sons, Wielkopolska was allotted to Prince Mieszko the Old. In 1247, it was subdivided into the provinces of Poznań and Kalisz. The last descendant of the Wielkopolska line of the Piasts, Przemysł II, reunited Wielkopolska in 1279, captured Cracow in 1290, inherited Eastern Pomerania and assumed the title of King of Poland in 1295. His murder a year later put an end to Wielkopolska's independence. From now on, rulers changed in rapid succession until Władysław the Elbow-High reunited Wielkopolska with the rest of Poland in 1314. Until the 18th century, it was one of the country's best developed regions. In 1772, its northern part was annexed by Prussia, and in 1793 the remaining part came under Prussian rule. It was only through the Wielkopolska Uprising (1918–1919) that almost the entire region was liberated and subsequently awarded to Poland by the Treaty of Versailles.

The neighbouring land of Kujawy, with its capital in Kruszwica, and later in Inowrocław, shared the historical vicissitudes of Wielkopolska. Today, both regions are traversed by many tourist routes and attract great numbers of visitors, who come to see the palaces, monasteries and museums, or just spend a quiet holiday on a farm, for there are still many places there free of the din and clatter of city life.

1. Reeds on Lake Gopło.
2. A Nativity scene from the Gniezno Codex.

GNIEZNO

Towards the end of the 8th century, a fortified settlement arose on a lakeside hillock named Góra Lecha. Timber-laced ramparts protected the heart of the Polanian state. The earliest document mentioning the name Gniezno dates from the 10th century – it was then the capital of what historians call the "Gniezno State". The first cathedral – possibly the same building whose remnants have now been discovered by archaeologists – was built on the initiative of Prince Mieszko I before 977, the year of the death of his wife Dąbrówka, who was buried there. In 979, the relics of the martyr St. Adalbert were also interred in the cathedral. A more sizeable church was erected during the reign of King Bolesław the Brave. In the year 1000, Gniezno was the venue for a meeting between Bolesław the Brave and Emperor Otto III, who recognised the Polish Prince as a sovereign ruler. Bolesław commemorated the occasion with a silver denarius bearing the proud inscription: Gnezdun civitas (Gniezno State). That same year an archbishopric was established in Gniezno, which became the first capital of the Polish state.

In 1018, part of the settlement and the entire cathedral burnt down, and Bolesław the Brave had a new one built in the final years of his life. The reconstructed cathedral saw two coronations in 1025: of Bolesław the Brave and of his son, Mieszko II. That was the climax of Gniezno's history. A mere twenty years later, the town and the Wielkopolska lands became engulfed in a pagan rebellion against Christianisation: the clergy were murdered, churches burnt down, and the Czech King Bretislav seized the opportunity to invade Poland and loot Gniezno, carrying away immense spoils, including St. Adalbert's relics. Reconstruction was sluggish and the town would never again be the capital of Poland. However, from the beginning of the 14th century, it was the coronation site of Polish kings. Gniezno received its municipal charter in 1239, but it did not succeed as a commercial centre due to strong competition from nearby Poznań. Since the Second World War, a comprehensive restoration programme has brought the town back to some of its former splendour.

1. *The Gothic Cathedral in Gniezno.*
2. *Chalice and Paten from Trzemeszno, ca. 1180; Archdiocesan Museum.*

➡ Ostrów Lednicki – an island on Lake Lednica where early Piast churches and a *palatium* have been unearthed (an archaeological reserve).

The most important historic monument in Gniezno is the cathedral, where relics dating back to the times of Mieszko I have been discovered. In place of the pre-Romanesque structure, Bolesław the Brave initiated the construction of a stone basilica with a twin-towered façade. However, there are few surviving remnants of this church.

The construction of the existing cathedral was undertaken by Archbishop Jarosław Bogoria Skotnicki (1342–1374). Deposited inside are St. Adalbert's relics, venerated since the 10th century and kept in a 17th-century Baroque reliquary. There are 14 chapels and several dozen tombs, including Primate Zbigniew Oleśnicki's epitaph by Veit Stoss (1495). Also housed in the cathedral are the treasury, archives and library – the collection includes liturgical vessels and illuminated codices. Set in the southern portal (the Kołudzki Chapel) is the bronze Gniezno Door from ca. 1170 – one of the peak achievements of Romanesque metalworking. Eighteen panels amid floral ornaments contain scenes from the life of St. Adalbert.

Gniezno cathedral is the official state cathedral and the seat of the Primate of Poland. This ecclesiastical title has been traditionally associated with the nation's oldest metropolitan see, whose incumbent enjoyed priority over the remaining metropolitans. The first Archbishop of Gniezno to be appointed Primate of Poland, in 1416, was Mikołaj Trąba. When Poland regained independence in 1918, a controversy ensued between Gniezno and Warsaw as to which of the two should be the Primate's seat; the dispute was solved in 1946 by way of joining the two sees in a personal union. This union was dissolved in 1992, but the Primate's office has remained with the Archbishop of Gniezno as the guardian of St. Adalbert's relics.

Gniezno is a pilgrimage site of nationwide importance. Its other historic buildings include the Romanesque Church of St. George from the 12th century and several Gothic churches from the 14th-16th centuries. There is also a museum devoted to the origins of the Polish state. Today, Gniezno – restored in preparation for the millennium of the meeting between Bolesław the Brave and Emperor Otto III – looks truly impressive.

1. The silver reliquary of St. Adalbert.
2. Detail of the bronze Gniezno Door.

➡ Dziekanowice – an open-air museum of folk architecture in picturesque lakeland scenery.

POZNAŃ

In the 10th century, Prince Mieszko I had his fortified settlement built on the island of Ostrów Tumski. During the Synod of Gniezno in the year 1000, the diocese of Poznań was set up for the missionary Bishop Unger. Destroyed during Bretislav's invasion of 1038, the town was rebuilt by Kazimierz the Restorer, who was buried in the reconstructed cathedral in 1058. Early trade was concentrated in Śródka, on the right bank of the Warta. In 1253, the left bank received a municipal charter based on Magdeburg Law. The right of storage granted by King Władysław Jagiełło in 1394 enabled the town to flourish. In 1519, a school known as the Lubrański Academy was established in Poznań, which disseminated Humanist ideas. Prosperity ended with the Swedish wars of the mid-17th century. The city began to recover a century later but development was interrupted by the annexation of Wielkopolska by the Prussians in 1793. In the 19th century, Poznań was a bastion of resistance against Germanisation. On 27 December 1918, a demonstration in support of Ignacy Jan Paderewski – a renowned pianist and politician, soon to become Prime Minister of the newly-independent Poland – turned into a revolt which soon engulfed Wielkopolska. In 1956, Poznań was the scene of violent clashes between workers and the police backed up by army units, with heavy casualties.

Poznań's historic monuments comprise, first and foremost, a medieval urban plan, including a delightful market square with a Renaissance town hall, as well as numerous residential houses and palaces from the 15th-18th centuries. The town hall, which now houses the city museum, was designed by Giovanni Battista Quadro in 1550–1560. It boasts a spectacular Great Hall from 1555, where the most important municipal celebrations were held. Outside, the characteristic arcaded loggia – together with parapets and sgraffito decoration – harmonises nicely with the Gothic tower.

An important Baroque landmark is the Jesuit church and college (where Chopin gave a performance in 1828), dating back to the second half of the 17th century. The most interesting accents of its interior are the polychro-

1. Poznań town hall.
2. The Great Hall.
3. Interior of St. Martin's Church.

➡ The 15th-cent. churches of St. Adalbert and the Calced Carmelites, the latter with an 18th-cent. chapel designed by Pompeo Ferrari.

me murals by Karl Dankwart and paintings by Szymon Czechowicz. Other worthwhile sites include the monumental Church of St. Stanislaus and the Church of St. Mary Magdalene. The more modern parts of the town abound in interesting examples of historicism and Art Nouveau.

The island of Ostrów Tumski lies between the Warta and its arm, the Cybina. In the latter part of the 10th century, a pre-Romanesque aisled cathedral was built in the lower part of the settlement. Archaeological excavations have uncovered a font and the remnants of two tombs, possibly of Mieszko I and Bolesław the Brave. It has also been hypothesised that a pre-Romanesque palatium with a chapel existed within the upper, fortified part of the settlement.

The most imposing of Poznań's churches is the Gothic cathedral from the 14th-15th centuries. It was built in stages. A twin-towered basilica was raised in 1346–1357, to which a chancel with an ambulatory and chapels were added before 1428. Most of its valuable furnishings and interior decorations were destroyed or lost during the Second World War. The precious, decorative bronze panels made by Nuremberg artists in the 15th century were found only in the 1990s – at the Hermitage in St. Petersburg.

Fortunately, wartime destruction did not affect the Golden Chapel. Built in 1834–1837 to the design of Francesco Maria Lanci, it is an interesting example of Romantic historicism, intended as a mausoleum of the early Piasts. The chapel's decorations comprise mosaics by Venetian artists, paintings by Oskar Sosnowski and January Suchodolski, and bronze statues of Mieszko I and Bolesław the Brave by the Berlin sculptor Christian Rauch. Another interesting chapel is that of the Blessed Sacrament with the multitiered tomb of the wealthy Górka family, the work of Geronimo Canavesi. The entrance to the Szołderski Chapel is decorated with late Gothic murals.

Other monuments on Ostrów Tumski include the Gothic collegiate church from the 15th century, the Lubrański Academy and a psalterists' house from 1512. The Archdiocesan Museum, established in 1936, has an exhibition of medieval scultpure (the highlight being a 14th-century Madonna in Majesty from Ołobok), as well as a collection of paintings, including *The Mourning of Christ* by Anton van Dyck and several funerary portraits of Polish noblemen.

1. Ostrów Tumski Cathedral.
2. Poznań Cathedral – the nave.
3. The Golden Chapel.

➡ St. Margaret's Church at Śródka (15th cent.); Dominican Church from 1244, remodelled in the 18th century; Dominican Nuns' Church (15th-16th cent.).

POZNAŃ

One of the most interesting episodes in the long history of Wielkopolska is the struggle that went on throughout the 19th century to uphold the national identity of the Polish population amid Prussian expansionism. "The longest war of modern Europe" was fought on the economic and cultural fronts, and it was the Poles, who persevered in pursuit of their cause in manor houses and peasant cottages alike, who emerged as winners. A special role in this struggle was played by the capital city of Wielkopolska.

Thus, a number of impressive public buildings were erected in Poznań over several decades; ideas of economic and cultural progress were advanced; civic and cultural institutions sprang up. Among the most important of these was the Raczyński Library (1829), one of Poland's oldest public libraries. In 1838–1841, the Bazar building was put up, soon to become a centre of Polish cultural and economic life. In 1858, a Society for the Advancement of Science was established, followed by a Society for Economic Development. The Prussian authorities, who carefully monitored developments in the city, concluded that the Poles were beginning to gain the upper hand and decided to react. In the space of barely a decade, they built the Kaiser Wilhelm Library (1902), Kaiser Friedrich Museum (1904), Royal Academy (1903), City Theatre (1910) and Colonisation Commission building (1908).

Nowadays, some of these edifices house academic institutions, libraries and museums. Among the latter, the National Museum plays a leading role, thanks to its magnificent collection of Polish and European painting, medieval art, and handicraft. The Neo-Renaissance building contains canvases by Jacek Malczewski, Józef Pankiewicz, Olga Boznańska, Władysław Podkowiński, Artur Nacht-Samborski and many others, as well as sculptures by Konstanty Laszczka and Xawery Dunikowski. A highlight of the museum is the Spanish masterpiece *Madonna of the Rosary* by Francisco de Zurbarán. The gallery of Romanesque and Gothic art comprises an extensive collection of Polish, Silesian, German and French sculpture, as well as panel painting.

1. *Jacek Malczewski, Poisoned Well I, National Museum, Poznań.*
2. *Church of St. John of Jerusalem.*

➡ The 19th-cent. citadel and city fortifications; Lake Malta with a regatta course; the nearby Romanesque Church of St. John.

ROGALIN

The Rogalin Protected Landscape Area encompasses extensive meadows and romantic oxbow lakes. In this beautiful scenery stands the part-Rococo, part-Classical Raczyński Palace. The family acquired Rogalin in the mid-18th century and the construction of the present palace, to the design of Ignacy Graff, was initiated in 1770 by Kazimierz Raczyński. Work was continued by his son Edward, who had the interiors of this magnificent, if somewhat heavy building decorated by Domenico Merlini and Jan Chrystian Kamsetzer.

In the first-floor ballroom – now called the Armoury – there is a collection of rare military exhibits, along with historical memorabilia and family heirlooms of the Raczyńskis. The southern annexe of the palace houses a museum of interiors, with a collection of old furniture and bric-a-brac. In the gallery building, put up in 1910, part of E. Raczyński's collection of Polish and European painting is shown, including canvases by Jan Matejko, Jacek Malczewski and Leon Wyczółkowski. The palace is approached from a forecourt, with stables and a paddock at its sides. In the coach-house, there is an interesting collection of carriages.

The chestnut-lined alley, the triple-arch bridge and the formal garden blend with the landscaped park. Together with the adjacent greens, they form a unique arboretum comprising 960 oak trees, varying in trunk circumference from 2 to 9 metres. The most famous of these is a cluster of three imposing trees named Lech, Czech and Rus, after the legendary founders of Poland, Bohemia and Ruthenia. In 1820, a mausoleum chapel, closely modelled on the Roman temple at Nîmes, was built at the edge of the park to house the burial crypt of the Raczyńskis.

Rogalin is but one example of Wielkopolska's awe-inspiring mansions, many of which have survived to this day. Another is found at Rydzyna, the grand residence of the Leszczyński and Sułkowski families, built on an artificial island surrounded with a moat and a beautiful park.

1. Rogalin oaks.
2. The Raczyński Palace at Rogalin.

➡ A 20th-cent. underground fortification system, now accessible to tourists; Łagów – a 14th-cent. castle of the Knights Hospitallers; Gościkowo – the Cistercian abbey.

KÓRNIK

Kórnik is one of those sites where an architectural monument vies for attention with its garden surroundings. Together with a large estate and, from 1458, the town, Kórnik was always in the possession of various eminent Wielkopolska families. First mentioned in 1362, it belonged, in turn, to the Górkas, Działyńskis and Zamoyskis. The island palace – the former Górka Castle – underwent complete remodelling in 184–1860 to the design of Karl Friedrich Schinkel, commissioned by Tytus Działyński. The German architect followed the contemporary vogue for romantic English Gothic. In accordance with the owner's wishes, the castle was adapted for use as a library and museum. It was given the look of a medieval fortress, with crenellated walls and towers, and a bridge across the moat.

Today, the restored interiors – including the remarkable Moresque Hall, now housing, among other things, a valuable collection of weaponry – contain furniture, paintings (e.g. by Artur Grottger, Jean-Pierre Norblin, Marcello Bacciarelli), handicraft, folk artefacts, hunting trophies and historical memorabilia. Kórnik is the only fully preserved magnate residence in Wielkopolska. Part of the castle is occupied by the library, holding one of Poland's most important collections of old manuscripts (e.g. by the Romantic poet Adam Mickiewicz), incunabula and books. The castle is also a monument to the life and work of Władysław Zamoyski. Having inherited Kórnik from the Działyńskis, he enlarged and modernised the residence.

In 1889, he bought a large part of the Tatra Mountains, saving it from devastation, and later bequeathed this land to the Polish nation, along with Kórnik castle and its museum collection. In accordance with Zamoyski's will, the property was to be administered by a specially established foundation. His bequest also included the famous arboretum founded in the 1830s by Tytus Działyński (taken over in 1953 by the Polish Academy of Sciences).

1. The Moresque Hall at Kórnik Castle.
2. The Neo-Gothic castle façade.

➡ Turew – the splendid 18th-cent. Chłapowski mansion (Baroque palace complex surrounded by a landscaped garden).

BISKUPIN

The history of Wielkopolska, Kujawy and Pałuki is even older than the early Piast state. In 1934, remnants of a large Lusatian stronghold, used in two periods between 700 and 440 BC, were found on an island on Lake Biskupińskie. It was an accidental discovery: a local schoolteacher – Walenty Szwejcer – was out collecting peat when he noticed some strange wooden structures sticking out of the mud.

The stronghold occupied an area of ca. 2 hectares. It had a compact, regular layout and was surrounded with a rampart. There were 13 rows of huts with 12 alleys in between, paved with timber. The dwellings were surrounded by a perimeter alley which followed the rampart. The fortifications consisted of a breakwater and a timber-laced rampart with a gate. Access to the island was provided by a wooden bridge. An estimated 1200 inhabitants lived in the settlement, deriving their livelihood from tilling the land, raising livestock, hunting and fishing.

Nowadays, Biskupin is an archaeological reserve and museum. Partial reconstruction of the settlement has been effected on the basis of excavation data, including the gate, ramparts, breakwater and two rows of huts. Traditional crops – barley, broad beans and lentils – are cultivated on specially arranged plots nearby. Archaeologists have reconstructed the old techniques of baking bread, firing earthenware and distilling wood tar. At the annual archaeological festival held at Biskupin, visitors can try their hand at making earthenware pots, hunting or steering a dugout. This is an unprecedented opportunity to get a first-hand experience of archaeology.

The site can be reached along the narrow-gauge railway running from Żnin to Gąsawa. Rail transport enthusiasts whose appetites have been whetted by the ride should visit the Narrow-Gauge Railway Museum at Wenecja. The reconstructed Biskupin settlement can also be admired from an excursion boat.

1. Biskupin – the reconstructed gate.
2. Reconstruction of the settlement.

➡ Lubostroń – the Neo-Classical Skórzewski palace surrounded by a large landscaped park; Żnin – a medieval town with the Pałuki Regional Museum.

KRUSZWICA AND TUM

Lake Gopło is a place where Polish legend and history meet. The lake, together with its picturesque surroundings, is part of the Millennium Park – a protected landscape area commemorating the ten centuries of Polish history. Kruszwica, situated on a peninsula jutting into the lake, is the legendary birthplace of the Piast dynasty: when an evil ruler named Popiel was allegedly devoured by mice, the good and just Piast Kołodziej ("Piast the Wheelwright") entered the scene, guided by angels, and assumed authority.

In the 8th-9th centuries, Kruszwica was indeed the centre of the tribal state of the Goplanie. In due time, the town built in the 10th-13th centuries received a municipal charter. Unfortunately, the 32-metre high, octagonal "Mouse Tower" – contrary to popular belief – is not the place where the villainous Popiel came to his sorry end. It is a remnant of a castle raised in the 14th century by Kazimierz the Great and destroyed by the Swedes three centuries later. In the 12th-15th centuries, the town was a major centre of glass and salt production. Kruszwica's oldest monument is the Romanesque collegiate church of SS. Peter and Paul from the first half of the 12th century, built of ashlars.

An equally imposing Romanesque church can be seen in the Łęczyca region, which borders Kujawy on the south. Its collegiate church, dedicated to the Blessed Virgin Mary and St. Alexius, was built in 1141–1161 on marshy land some distance away from the ducal (later royal) town of Łęczyca. This is a fairly impressive structure: an aisled basilica with two choirs. It is flanked by four towers on the outside – two square and two cylindrical – contributing to the fortress-like appearance of the church. Remodelled towards the end of the 15th century and in the 18th century, and subsequently bombed and destroyed by fire in September 1939, the church was restored to its original Romanesque form after the war (work was completed in 1961). Inside are fragments of Romanesque, Gothic and Renaissance polychrome decoration, a Romanesque portal and Baroque furnishings.

1. The "Mouse Tower" on Lake Gopło.
2. The collegiate church at Tum near Łęczyca.

➡ Ciechocinek – a spa with an early-19th-cent. saltworks; Inowrocław – the 12th cent. Romanesque Church of the Blessed Virgin Mary, spa park.

STRZELNO

The "Piast Trail" that winds its way across the Kujawy region passes through Strzelno, one of the most interesting Romanesque complexes in Poland. Held initially by the Canons Regular from nearby Trzemeszno, Strzelno later passed to the Premonstratensian convent, founded – in all probability – by Piotr Wszeborowic of the Łabędź clan, Castellan of Kruszwica and subsequently Palatine of Kujawy. From the 12th to the 18th century, the town was the property of the Premonstratensian nuns. The most valuable historic monuments in town are two early-Romanesque churches from the 12th century on St. Adalbert's Hill. The Holy Trinity Church, formerly a monastery church, has acquired in the aftermath of much remodelling the appearance of an aisled basilica with a Baroque façade and spires. It may not look particularly promising on the outside, but inside, a priceless gem of mediaeval art had been hidden for centuries. In 1946, sculpted Romanesque columns were discovered, which now count among the most precious relics of the period. They have survived because they were covered with brickwork in the course of Baroque-style remodelling – apparently, the vogue for Romanesque art had not begun yet. The sculptures on two of the columns represent personifications of virtues (south column) and vices (north column). Adjoining the church to the north is the 15th-century, heavily remodelled convent. At some point the nuns likewise opted for fashionable, Baroque decorations and had the old details plastered over. In 1953, a magnificent Romanesque tympanum was uncovered in a small room located at the former entrance to the church. It shows the figure of Christ which must have crowned a 13th-century portal. Not far from the convent is a stone rotunda, with a tower and a square chancel, dating back to the turn of the 12th century. This little church is dedicated to St. Procopius. Its dome-shaped vault, supported by massive ribs, has been preserved to this day. The nave is separated from the tower by a Romanesque biforate window divided by a slender column; in other narrow Romanesque windows there are stylised stained-glass decorations. Preserved from the original furnishing is a stone font.

1. *Interior of the Holy Trinity Church at Strzelno with one of the famous columns.*
2. *Rotunda of St. Procopius.*

➡ Włocławek – the Gothic Cathedral of the Assumption (14th-15th cent.); historic houses and granaries; Museum of the Kujawy and Dobrzyń Lands.

ŁÓDŹ

In the Łęczyca region, on the fringe of historic Wielkopolska, a most unusual city arose in the 19th century. Few other cities have ever seen such rapid and at the same time stormy development as Łódź. It was the product of an economic boom reminiscent of the Klondike gold rush, rather than deliberate efforts at town planning. First mentioned in the 14th century, Łódź remained for many years a small settlement in the Bishop's possession, inhabited by farmers. When church land was confiscated in the 19th century, the authorities turned Łódź into a colony for immigrant weavers from Silesia, Wielkopolska and Germany. Among the newcomers, a special role was to be played by Ludwig Geyer from Saxony, considered to be the father of modern weaving and spinning in the Łódź area. In 1823, construction of the district known as Nowe Miasto was commenced, and by 1828 a sizeable settlement had risen along the Piotrków-Łęczyca road, specialising in cotton and linen production. In 1837, power looms and a 50-HP steam engine were installed at Geyer's factory. By 1850, the latter had a workforce of 650 and turned out half a million roubles worth of merchandise a year. A breakthrough came with the abolition of tariffs between the Russian-dominated Kingdom of Poland and Czarist Russia, which opened the way for the expansion of percale exports to the east. To meet the growing demand, enormous factories were established, e.g., the ones owned by K. Scheibler, L. Grohman and I.K. Poznański. A caste of German and Jewish multi-millionaires, popularly named *Lodzermenschen*, had emerged. Capital accumulation attracted banks and credit institutions to the city. The attractiveness of Łódź as a manufacturing and commercial centre further increased in 1866, when the city received its first railway connection. Fields and wastelands were built up with factories, office buildings, workers' homes (for instance, the modern Księży Młyn housing estate designed by Hilary Majewski) and slums. The epitome of progress was the Grand Hotel from the first years of the 20th century, equipped with air conditioning, in-room telephones, an air-ozonisation system and cinema. The hotel is situated on Piotrkowska Street, which is now the city's principal shopping area, with many bars and restaurants.

1. *Department store in Piotrkowska Street.*
2. *Intricate Art Nouveau forms in Łódź.*
3. *Art Nouveau stained glass in L. Kindermann's villa.*

➡ Łęczyca – the early Baroque Bernardine Church; Sieradz – the medieval town plan with a market square and streets intersecting at right angles.

In no other town of the Kingdom of Poland was the contrast between extreme luxury and utter poverty so conspicuous. Countless legends circulated about Łódź's factory owners and their residences, including stories of ballroom floors tiled with gold roubles. The weaving-industry tycoons could afford anything. Eloquent evidence of the amounts of money involved (although not exactly of good taste) is provided by the palaces built for I. K. Poznański. His imposing residence at Gdańska Street, built in 1910, now houses the Academy of Music. Another palace, dubbed "the Louvre of Łódź" for its enormous opulence, is now the seat of the city's Historical Museum. It is definitely worth visiting, if for nothing else than to see the fabulously rich interiors decorated in historicist or Art Nouveau style. Yet another of Poznański's palaces has now been converted into an interesting Art Museum, with an extensive gallery of painting and a good collection of Art Nouveau glassware. Other industrial magnates kept pace with Poznański. Leading architects (e.g. Hilary Majewski, Adolf Seligson) were commissioned to build the grand residences, whose designs impress even today, as do the huge, neo-Renaissance factory buildings.

More human proportions were maintained in the case of the Kindermann villa, designed in Art Nouveau style by Gustaw Landau-Gauteger. The same architect was the author of many other attractive and fanciful designs from the early years of the 20th century. Łódź provides an ample basis for comparison in this field, as the vicinity of Piotrkowska Street is Poland's largest preserved complex of Art Nouveau architecture.

While strolling past the mansions and relishing their curvilinear, floral ornaments and eclectic exuberance, it is worthwhile stopping in at the Museum of Textiles to learn how, in the spinning and weaving mills of Łódź, cotton and flax were turned into a river of gold, a fraction of which was enough to transform wastelands into a thriving town in a matter of decades. Nowadays, you may or may not like Łódź, but it certainly will not leave you indifferent. The factories, offices and residential buildings remain the most impressive and enduring monument to 19th-century Polish capitalism.

1

2

3

1. *Karol Hiller*, Rain, *Art Museum, Łódź.*
2. *Gable at No. 43 Piotrkowska Street.*
3. *Gable at No. 128 Piotrkowska Street.*

➡ Kalisz – a town included in Ptolemy's map from the 2nd cent., with many historic buildings, such as the Archbishops' Palace, town hall and collegiate Church of the Blessed Virgin Mary.

TRZEMESZNO, MOGILNO, LĄD

Wielkopolska has a lot to offer to the visitor, yet the most impressive sites are the old churches and monasteries, where time seems to stand still. One such place is the church in Trzemeszno in the Gniezno Lakeland, which belonged, in turn, to the Benedictines (who had come from Tyniec), the Canons Regular and, finally, the local parish. It is a stone basilica with a pre-Romanesque crypt from 996, rebuilt in Romanesque style in ca. 113–1145. The entire structure underwent thorough Baroque remodelling in 1782–1791.

Not far away lies Mogilno, a settlement that grew around the Benedictine abbey established in 1065 by King Bolesław the Bold. The Gothic church from the second half of the 16th century has some 11th-century detailing, as well as two Romanesque crypts. Preserved in the western crypt is one of the first vaults ever built in Poland – supported at the centre on a single pillar. Originally, the church had a transept with two apses. The interior has undergone transformations, too. In late Gothic times it received net and cellular vaults, while the Baroque and Rococo contribution includes the furnishings and an impressive high altar. An addition from 1797 was the monumental façade with towers. The monastery buildings have been remodelled and transformed on several occasions, which, however, does not detract from their beauty.

Ląd used to be one of the principal centres of Wielkopolska and the seat of Prince Mieszko the Old, who brought the Cistercians there in 1145. The abbey was dissolved by the Russian authorities in 1819. In 1850–1864, the monastery was taken over by the Capuchins, and since 1921 it has belonged to the Salesians. The complex consists of a church dedicated to the Blessed Virgin Mary and St. Nicholas (Romanesque, remodelled 17th-18th centuries in Baroque style) and a part-Gothic, part-Baroque monastery. The church is covered by an imposing 38-metre high dome designed by Pompeo Ferrari. Inside, the church is richly decorated with stuccoes, sculptures and paintings. The oratory with heraldic murals (before 1375) is one of the highest-ranking monuments of medieval art in Poland.

1. The ecclesiastical complex at Ląd.
2. Dome of the Canons Regular Church at Trzemeszno.
3. The Benedictine Abbey at Mogilno.

➡ Gołuchów Castle in French Renaissance style (1560), situated in Wielkopolska's largest protected landscape area; a collection of antique vases.

MAZOVIA AND PODLASIE

For centuries, strong Mazovian separatism accounted for the scepticism of local rulers about joining the other Polish provinces in a union. The Mazovians, flanked by the Poles on the one side and by Baltic tribes on the other, made a point of maintaining their separate identity. In the early 13th century, the province, together with neighbouring Kujawy, came under the rule of Konrad of Mazovia, who intended to unite the remaining parts of Poland around his principality. Yet these plans came to grief and in 1248 Kujawy seceded from Mazovia and became further divided in 1262 into the Lands of Płock and Czersk. The political developments of the century made Mazovia an arena of rivalry and wars between Poland, Bohemia and the Teutonic Knights. In 1351–1355, Mazovia was Poland's fief and part of its territory was controlled by King Kazimierz the Great. Reunited in 1370 under Siemowit III, it regained independence, although its links with Poland were restored under the reign of Władysław Jagiełło. The last of the Mazovian princes, Janusz, was poisoned in 1526, and his land was incorporated into Poland.

Podlasie, originally inhabited by the pagan Jatzvingians, had been an expansion target for Kievan Rus' since the 11th century, and afterwards it became an object of rivalry between the Polish Crown, Mazovia and Lithuania. It was only through the Union of Lublin (1569) that almost the entire province ended up within Poland's borders. The convoluted history of the region is reflected in its present-day ethnic composition: Poles, Lithuanians, Belarussians and Tartars have been living there side by side for centuries.

The misty landscape of the Mazovia plains, crossed by river valleys and meandering streams, exudes a moody and nostalgic aura. In the east, the vast fields lined with willow trees blend into the woodlands of Podlasie. Those beautiful forests are but an echo of the immense woods that once covered the entire Polish-Lithuanian borderland. One of their relics is the regal Białowieża Forest. In the woodland wilderness, or in the undulating morainic landscape of northern Mazovia, oases of perfect peace and quiet are still to be found.

1. Mazovian landscape.
2. Statue of King Zygmunt III atop a column in Warsaw.

WARSAW

On 17 September 1939, German incendiary bombs set fire to the Royal Castle in Warsaw. Even though the rescue operation, hampered by diving Luftwaffe bombers, succeeded in putting out the flame, the losses were incalculable. But that was only the beginning.

Unlike Poznań, Gniezno or Cracow, Warsaw has no ancient roots. It was first mentioned in documents only in the early 14th century. However, its central location was an asset that Polish monarchs came to appreciate in time. The modest ducal residence was gradually enlarged into a magnificent edifice. It was especially to the Vasa dynasty that Warsaw Castle owed its enhancement, and King Zygmunt III's decision in 1596 to transfer the royal court from Wawel to Mazovia became a turning point in Warsaw's history. Poland's rulers took great care in improving their new seat, and to this end enlisted the services of the best architects, including Giovanni Trevano, Matteo Castelli, Constantino Tencalla, Agostino Vicenze Locci. The castle – like the city's other mansions – was totally devastated in the times of the "Swedish Deluge" and restored during the reign of Jan III Sobieski. But not for long. In 1704, the Swedes stormed Warsaw again, destroying part of the castle. Renovation and remodelling lasted throughout the 18th century. The castle owed its new shape above all to King Stanisław August Poniatowski – a mediocre ruler but a great connoisseur and patron of art. To be sure, critics blamed the King for extravagance, claiming that the amounts spent without adequate planning on the reconstruction effort would have been sufficient to build four other castles from scratch, but the work of Giacopo Fontana, Domenico Merlini and Jan Chrystian Kamsetzer was breathtaking in its effect. This was complemented by the exquisite art collection built up by the King, including goldwork, statues and paintings (among others, by Marcello Bacciarelli, Canaletto and Jan Bogumił Plersch). But first and foremost, the castle was in those years the arena of a battle for the future of Poland and the scene of a belated attempt to avert her impending fall – it was here that the Constitution of 3 May 1791 was adopted.

1. Zamkowy Square with the Royal Castle and Zygmunt Column.
2. The Throne Room at the Royal Castle.

➡ The Baroque "Tin-roofed" Palace, 17th cent.; Krakowskie Przedmieście Street.

During the era of Partitions, the castle fell into disrepair. Only in 1917 did the Regency Council inaugurate its sessions in the ballroom, and on 11 November 1918 the white-and-red flag was flown from the castle tower – a symbol of an independent Poland reclaiming the castle, the capital city and the state. After renovation, part of the building was used as apartments for luminaries of culture and science. In 1926, the castle became the official residence of the President of the Republic. In 1944, after the defeat of the Warsaw Uprising, the destructive frenzy of the Nazis surpassed even the damage done by Brandenburg, the Swedes, and the Muscovites combined. As if looting were not enough, they literally razed the castle to the ground (as they did the entire Old Town) using high explosives. The decision to rebuild the castle was taken immediately after the war, but its was not put into practice until the early 1970s. Today, the castle is once again the pride of the Polish capital. Meticulously restored, it provides an apt setting for the growing collection of Polish art displayed in its chambers.

In front of the castle, in the middle of Zamkowy Square, from which the elegant Krakowskie Przedmieście and Miodowa Street begin, stands Poland's oldest monument to a layman. King Władysław IV thus paid homage to his father, Zygmunt III, in 1644. The column was designed by Constantino Tencalla and the statue was cast in bronze by Clementi Molli.

Abutting on Zamkowy Square is the densely built-up Old Town, at the centre of which is the picturesque Market Square. Rebuilt from scratch after the war, it has been entered onto UNESCO's World Heritage List as a unique example of comprehensive reconstruction and restoration of an entire urban complex. The most important monuments in the Old Town include the 14th-century basilican cathedral with the tombs of several celebrated Poles. Also to be seen in the cathedral are the Baroque Baryczka Chapel with a miraculous 16th-century crucifix, and the epitaphs of the last Mazovian dukes. The Hanseatic-type brick residential houses from the 15th-16th centuries with late Gothic and late Renaissance elements are best exemplified by the Falkiewicz, Pod Murzynkiem and Fukier Houses in the Market Square. Surrounding the Old Town is a ring of reconstructed walls with a 15th-16th-century Barbican. The picturesque Kamienne Schodki ("Stone Steps") descend towards the Vistula, while Krzywe Koło ("Crooked Circle") Street leads to the Mermaid monument – the emblem of Warsaw.

1. *Conference room at the Royal Castle.*
2. *Old Town Market Square, with the cathedral spire in the background.*

➡ The Neo-Classical Grand Theatre (19th cent.); Revenue and Treasury Commission building (19th cent.); Lutheran church at Trzech Krzyży Square.

WARSAW

Łazienki is a charming palace in park surroundings, situated in the district of Ujazdów. In the second half of the 17th century, Tylman van Gameren built a Baroque pavilion on a rectangular island for the Grand Marshal of the Crown, Herakliusz Lubomirski. In 1764, the entire property was bought by Stanisław August Poniatowski, who had the park rearranged and new pavilions constructed. In 1772, major remodelling began, aiming to transform Łazienki into the King's summer residence, a task which took 20 years to complete. The external appearance of the building, thereafter called Palace on the Water, was radically altered – in Neo-Classical style. Among the architects and artists commissioned to do the task were Domenico Merlini, Jan Chrystian Kamsetzer and Jan Bogumił Plersch. The arrangement of Łazienki Park – following the model of English landscape gardens – was designed by Johann Christian Schuch. The design incorporated a number of buildings, such as the Myślewicki Palace, Stara Pomarań-czarnia ("Old Orangery") – which now houses Poland's largest museum of sculpture – and the beautiful Island Theatre. A monument to Chopin was put up in 1926 by the pond. The Palace on the Water survived almost unchanged until 1939. In 1944, the Germans set fire to the residence, gutting its interiors, but, luckily, it was not blown up.

Behind The Palace on the Water is the Military School Building from which the young insurgents marched on the Belvedere Palace – the residence of the Czar's brother, the Grand Duke Constantine – on a fateful night in 1830, which marked the outbreak of the November Uprising. The Belvedere was originally a small palace built in 1659 for Chancellor Krzysztof Pac. Remodelled in the 18th and 19th centuries, it found favour with various rulers of Poland. From 1818, it was the headquarters of the Grand Duke Constantine, and after independence, the residence of Józef Piłsudski, who died there on 12 May 1935. During the Second World War, the building was converted into a residence for Hans Frank and survived the war. In 1945–1952, it was the official seat of Bolesław Bierut (the puppet President of Poland after the communist takeover) and afterwards – of several Chairmen of the Council of State.

1. *Dining room with a statue of Aphrodite.*
2. *The Palace on the Water.*

➡ The Ogród Saski ("Saxon Gardens") designed by Tylman van Gameren in the 17th cent.; Ujazdów Castle and Park (18th cent.), now a Gallery of Modern Art.

The greatest attraction of suburban Wilanów is the sumptuous palace built for King Jan III Sobieski in place of the former Leszczyński Palace from the first half of the 17th century. Subsequently, the palace belonged to the Sieniawski, Czartoryski, Lubomirski, Potocki and Branicki families. Sobieski – Poland's last warrior-king – sought rest there after the Relief of Vienna in 1683. In the Polish tradition, Sobieski is equated with the flamboyant "Sarmatian" tradition, which was cherished by the greater part of the nobility.

Many of Wilanów's chambers and furnishings are intimately connected with the King and his beloved French wife Marie-Casimire, affectionately called Marysieńka. The most spectacular interiors are the royal couple's living quarters, the Etruscan Room, the Grand Crimson Chamber and the garden gallery. Some of these are decorated with murals by the King's protégé, Jerzy Eleuter Siemiginowski. The artist also executed a number of plafond paintings and several portraits of the monarch and his family. Another bedchamber plafond, the beautiful Eos, was painted by Jan Reiser, who showed the goddess *déshabillée* with the face of the pretty queen. The palace, whose two wings encompass a spacious courtyard, was built around 1680 to the design of Agostino Vicenze Locci, enlarged in 1692 and remodelled in 1722–1725 (Giovanni Spazzio), 1730–1733 (Johann Sigismund Deybel) and 1848 (Francesco Maria Lanci).

The palace is surrounded with a formal garden from 1682, supplemented in 1799–1801 with landscaped sections. It is dotted with Romantic pavilions (designed by Chrystian Piotr Aigner). To the fore of the palace is the Neo-Gothic Potocki Mausoleum designed in 1832 by Henryk Marconi, with sculptures by Jakub Tatarkiewicz and K. Hegel. The remaining components of the palace complex are St. Anne's Church from 1857–1870 and auxiliary buildings.

During the Second World War, the art collection was plundered by the Nazis, who also devastated the park. Fortunately, most of the missing works of art were later recovered. After restoration, the palace became a branch of the National Museum and a modern pavilion hidden behind the façade of the old riding-school houses an interesting Poster Museum.

1. Wilanów Palace.
2. Queen Marysieńka's bedchamber.

➡ Palace of Science and Culture – at 234.5 metres, this huge Socialist Realist edifice dominates the Warsaw skyline; buildings in Constitution Square.

WARSAW

Warsaw is renowned for its excellent museums, the most important of which is the National Museum. Its beginnings date back to 1862, and it is now the largest institution of this type in Poland. Formerly known as the Fine Arts Museum, it received its current name in 1916. Nowadays, it is housed in an International-Style building on Aleje Jerozolimskie, constructed in 1926–1938 to the design of Tadeusz Tołwiński and Antoni Dygat. During the Second World War, the Museum building was damaged and the collection was plundered and taken away to the Reich by the Nazis.

The exhibits are arranged into sections: antiquity (Egyptian, Greek, Etruscan, Roman and Byzantine art; since 1964, the highlight has been a collection of murals from Faras in Egypt), foreign art (Flemish, Dutch and French painting from the 15th-19th centuries; sculpture from the 15th-19th centuries), medieval art, Polish art of the 16th-19th centuries, decorative art, art of the Far and Middle East, and modern art. There are also separate exhibition rooms devoted to drawing and engraving, miniature and numismatics. In 1992, a new exhibition of Polish painting was opened; the collection numbers 7,000 works by Polish painters and foreign artists who worked in Poland. The National Museum has a number of branches, comprising: Łazienki Palace and Park, Wilanów Palace and Park, Poster Museum at Wilanów, Arkadia Park, Nieborów Palace, Museum of Łowicz, Xawery Dunikowski Museum, Museum of Ignacy Jan Paderewski and the Polish Emigration in America and Krośniewice Museum. One of the wings of the Museum's main building is occupied by the Polish Military Museum, which documents the long-standing tradition of the Polish armed forces. The tragic and heroic moments in Warsaw's history are commemorated at the Warsaw Citadel Museum, Museum of "Pawiak" Prison, and the Museum of the Jewish Historical Institute, which documents, among other things, the tragic fate of the uprising in the Warsaw ghetto in 1943.

Warsaw also has a number of art galleries, among which a special place is occupied by the "Zachęta". Its name (meaning "Encouragement") was derived from the "Society for the Encouragement of Fine Arts", which functioned in Warsaw from 1860 to 1939. Its seat at Małachowski Square was the venue of many individual and group exhibitions, as well as the annual salons held from 1904. The Society acted as an intermediary between artists and patrons, developed its own collection, and financed art scholarships. Nowadays, "Zachęta" House accommodates the Gallery of Modern Art.

1. *Jan Matejko,* The Battle of Grunwald, *National Museum in Warsaw.*
2. *Olga Boznanska,* Grandma's Name Day, *National Museum in Warsaw.*

➡ Tomb of the Unknown Soldier in a surviving fragment of arcades from the Saski Palace; Baroque Church of the Nuns of the Visitation; Neo-Classical Holy Cross Church (housing an urn with Frédéric Chopin's heart).

PŁOCK

The town of Płock owed its early development to the patronage of Prince Władysław Herman, who promoted this Mazovian ducal seat to the rank of capital of the Piast domain in 1079. There is no way of telling whether he was attracted by the picturesque, steep Vistula bank, or by the more practical considerations of easy access to Mazovia, Kujawy and Wielkopolska. A bishopric had already been established in Płock by King Bolesław the Bold. The cathedral, built towards the end of the 11th century, was the place of Władysław Herman's burial in 1102, and in 1138 it received the remains of King Bolesław the Wry-mouthed. After 1127, the construction of the so-called "second cathedral" was commenced by Bishop Alexander of Malonne, the founder of Czerwińsk abbey, who commissioned a magnificent bronze door for the Płock cathedral. This masterpiece of Romanesque art featured numerous allegorical scenes, Biblical themes, complex symbols and effigies of bishops. It was presented by Prince Bolesław the Curly to the Sophia monastery in Novgorod, where it has remained since the end of the 14th century. The present cathedral was founded by Bishop Andrzej Krzycki. Built in 1532–1534 in the direct vicinity of the castle, it replaced the older church. Many valuable objects of art have been preserved at the cathedral, the most outstanding of which is a medieval herm representing St. Sigismund. It is crowned with a diadem originating from the second quarter of the 13th century. Other highlights of the cathedral treasury include a chalice with a paten donated by Prince Konrad of Mazovia, and illuminated medieval manuscripts. The former Benedictine monastery facing the cathedral now houses the Mazovian Museum, with Poland's largest collection of Art Nouveau handicraft.

1. Herm of St. Sigismund in the cathedral treasury.
2. Płock Cathedral.

➡ Pułtusk – Bishops' Castle and ecclesiastical buildings, with the collegiate church dedicated to the Annunciation and to St. Matthew; Czerwinsk – 12th-cent. monastery of the Canons Regular.

ŻELAZOWA WOLA

The village of Żelazowa Wola on the Utrata River, lost amid the Mazovian plains at the edge of Kampinos Forest, will always be remembered as the birthplace of a musical genius. It was here, in an annexe to Skarbek Palace, that Frédéric Chopin was born. The palace itself burnt down during the First World War, but the annexe, built in the first years of the 19th century, survived and was renovated in 1930–1931. Lech Niemojewski gave it the appearance of a Neo-Classical manor house, now overgrown with vine. It is surrounded by a scenic garden, rearranged in 1933–1935, in which a monument to the composer has been put up. The stylish manor interiors house a modest Chopin Museum. During the summer season, piano concerts are held there.

Frédéric Chopin (1810–1849) did not spend much time at Żelazowa Wola: he spent his early days in Warsaw, where he began to learn the piano, composing his first polonaise at the age of seven. From 1818, he gave public performances, and was hailed as a prodigy by the Warsaw salons. During summer vacations, he became acquainted with the folklore and music of Mazovia, Wielkopolska, and the Lublin region. On 2 November 1830, he left Warsaw for Paris, where he settled for good.

Chopin's oeuvre consists mostly of solo pieces for piano (including 27 etudes, 16 polonaises and 57 mazurkas). The hallmark of his music is the blend of virtuoso style with Polish musical tradition, including folk music. His unequalled mazurkas and polonaises epitomised for decades the national style in Polish music. When the composer died in Paris, the poet Cyprian Kamil Norwid, who often saw him in the last months of his life, wrote in Chopin's obituary: "He was a Varsovian by birth, a Pole from the heart, and his talent made him a citizen of the world."

The most splendid tribute to Chopin's greatness is the prestigious Chopin Piano Competition, held regularly since 1927.

1. Żelazowa Wola – the birthplace of Frédéric Chopin.
2. Interior of the Chopin manor house.

➡ Modlin – an early-19th-century fortress with a barracks over 2 kilometres long; Palmiry in the Kampinos Forest – the site of mass executions by the Nazis.

ARKADIA AND NIEBORÓW

Arkadia is proof that vision combined with money can transform the Mazovian plain into an ancient Paradise. The park – planned in a Romantic spirit in the then fashionable Anglo-Chinese style – was established by Princess Helena Radziwiłł on her estate extending between Łowicz and Nieborów in 1778–1821. Her vision turned into reality thanks to Szymon Bogumił Zug and Wojciech Jaszczołd. Both the name and layout of the park are a reference to the traditions of Antiquity: Arcadia was the mythical country extolled by Virgil's bucolics as an ideal of simple and good life. In the Arkadia Park, Neo-Classical motifs harmonise with the Romantic landscaping. Riverside pastures and woods were incorporated into the park's layout, featuring meadows, a pond and a hill. The structures erected in the park draw on both ancient tradition (Elysian Fields, Temple of Diana – 1783, hippodrome, aqueduct – 1784) and Romantic inspiration (Gothic House and Gallery – before 1800, Archpriest's House – 1783), and make ample use of earlier stone fragments of both Classical and domestic provenance. The latter comprise, for instance, details from St. Victoria's Chapel in the collegiate church at Łowicz, including fragments of stone sculpture by Jan Michałowicz. Arkadia undoubtedly ranks among the most beautiful parks in Poland.

Not far from Arkadia lies Nieborów, a Baroque palace also surrounded by a park, built in 1690–1699 as a residence for Primate Michał Radziejowski. The palace was designed by Tylman van Gameren, and the other buildings of the complex (including the orangeries) – by Szymon Bogumił Zug (end of the 18th century). In 1881, the Radziwiłł family began manufacturing faience and majolica in a former brewery. Their factory remained in operation (with some interruptions) until 1906. Its products constitute the core of the exhibition shown in the palace – now the property of the National Museum. The surviving part of the original Radziwiłł collection includes paintings from their gallery, a valuable library and a collection of sculpture.

1. Temple of Diana in the Arkadia Park.
2. Stone details at Arkadia.

➡ Łowicz – the former site of the Primate's residence with a preserved historic urban plan and churches; Krośniewice – the Jerzy Dunin-Borkowski collection.

PUŁAWY

The town of Puławy on the Vistula occupies a very special place in Polish culture. It is the place where the idea of the modern museum and the vogue for national memorabilia originated in Poland. In the 17th century, Puławy was the residence of Herakliusz Lubomirski. In 1736, Aleksander August Czartoryski turned the palace into a forum of political debate. Afterwards, the estate passed to Adam Kazimierz Czartoryski, the commander of the Cadet Corps, and his wife Izabela née Fleming. After the defeat of the Kościuszko Insurrection of 1794, the Czartoryskis were punished by the Czarina Catherine II with the destruction of their palace, but in 1796 they returned to their residence, as it now lay within the Habsburg realm!

Thanks to Princess Czartoryska, Puławy once again became a repository for the gems of Polish culture, which Izabela amassed with the greatest passion. To house these items she had Chrystian Piotr Aigner build several pavilions in the park, the most famous of which are the Temple of the Sibyl (a replica of the Vesta Temple from Tivoli, 1798-1801) and Gothic House (1809). Her private collection was a mishmash of invaluable cultural relics, outstanding works of art and utter rubbish. Pride of place went to royal memorabilia – Władysław Jagiełło's sword, Stefan Bathory's and Jan III Sobieski's sabres, as well as watches, rings and chains. The exhibits also included – apart from the (supposed) skeleton of Bolesław the Brave – also Hetman Stefan Czarniecki's knuckle, Queen Jadwiga's shoe, the earthly remains of Nicolaus Copernicus and the head of Hetman Stefan Żółkiewski! The Puławy estate was confiscated by the Russian authorities after the defeat of the November Uprising in 1831, but the collection was salvaged and safely transferred to Paris, and from there – decades later – to Cracow. The abandoned palace became a girls' lycée (relocated from Warsaw), while Puławy was renamed New Alexandria by the Russians.

1. The Czartoryski Palace at Puławy.
2. Temple of the Sibyl.

➡ Lubartów – Sanguszko Palace, Baroque parish church, Capuchin church and monastery; Kock – wartime cemetery of the "Polesie" operations unit, Neo-Classical Jabłonowski Palace from the 18th cent.

BIAŁYSTOK AND TYKOCIN

The Knyszyn Forest – the favourite hunting ground of the Jagiellons – adjoins the outskirts of Białystok, which has grown from a small, provincial town into the largest and most important city of northeastern Poland. Białystok rose in importance when it became the seat of Jan Klemens Branicki (1689–1771), the last member of the Gryf clan. Mediocre as a military commander – despite his rank of Hetman – and inept as a politician, Branicki was nevertheless praised for the skilful management of his estates and for refined artistic tastes. He had lived in France for many years and transplanted to Podlasie the architectural designs he had seen there. Sycophants called his Białystok palace the "Versailles of Podlasie" – with some exaggeration, to be sure – and the contented magnate rewarded them with rings and snuffboxes. The late Baroque palace and park complex lies at the heart of the Old Town in present-day Białystok. Branicki commissioned Johann Sigismund Deybel and Jan Henryk Klemm to remodel and enlarge the residence in 1728–1758. The result was a spacious palace with a number of courtyards, surrounded by a formal garden – currently, it serves as the seat of the Białystok Medical Academy.

Nearby Tykocin used to be the country's main arsenal, and although it never lost the municipal charter it received in 1424, it is now only a village in the Biebrza Basin. During the Second World War, more than half of Tykocin's inhabitants perished. The Nazis murdered its Jewish community, which had lived there since the reign of King Jan Olbracht. The 17th-century Baroque synagogue is now a Museum of Jewish Culture. In the medieval Market Square stands a monument from 1763, commemorating the former owner of Tykocin, Hetman Stefan Czarniecki. Other interesting sites include the 18th-century Holy Trinity Church and the late Baroque Bernardine church with a former monastery.

1. Interior of the Tykocin synagogue.
2. The Branicki Palace in Białystok.

➡ Fortified Orthodox Church of Annunciation; 16th-cent. Basilian Friars' monastery with magnificent murals; Archimandrites' Palace from the 17th-18th cent., now a museum.

THE BIAŁOWIEŻA FOREST

This immense tract of woodland probably owes its name to the Biała Wieża ("White Tower") which can still be seen at Kamieniec Litewski. The forest occupies the eastern part of the Bialska Plain. It has a total area of ca. 128,000 hectares, of which 58,000 hectares lies in Poland. Due to its unique natural features, the Białowieża National Park, has been declared a biosphere reserve. Various types of woodland are present in the Białowieża Forest – mixed forest with a preponderance of oak, hornbeam and spruce, pine-and-spruce forests, marshy coniferous forests and ash-and-alder carrs. In the strict reserve, there exist about 800 species of higher plants, 400 moss and lichen species, and more than 1000 species of fungi. The fauna includes the European bison, elk, beaver, wolf, lynx, black grouse, black stork, eagle-owl and mud turtle. Two of the rarest species – the European bison (in 1919, it was close to extinction) and the *tarpan* – a Polish breed of a small and sturdy wild horse – are bred in special forest farms. The animal population of the Białowieża Forest needs to be increased in view of the serious depletion of game caused by excessive hunting over the centuries. A stone obelisk in Nowa Białowieża on the Narewka River commemorates a particularly big kill made by hunters in September 1752.

The Podlasie region is a melting pot of cultures. Grabarka is the main Orthodox pilgrimage destination in Poland. It is located at a site where the local population was miraculously saved from a cholera epidemic in 1710: the people took refuge on a nearby hill and drank water from a spring on its slope. Until recently, a wooden Church of the Transfiguration (1789) stood at the top of Penitent Hill. Unfortunately, it burnt down in 1990 and has now been rebuilt in brick. Nearby is a small Panagia Church, used in winter, and the only Orthodox convent in Poland, dedicated to SS. Martha and Mary, surrounded with hundreds of votive crosses. Podlasie is also home to Poland's Tartar population, settled there in the 15th century by the Lithuanian Prince Witold. The Tartars formed light cavalry units and were known for their loyalty to the Crown. Their descendants can be met today, for instance, in the villages of Bohoniki and Kruszyniany. These two villages have mosques and Moslem cemeteries.

1. Bison in the Białowieża Forest.
2. Forest wilderness.
3. Ancient Białowieża woodland.

➡ Kodeń – the 17th cent. Shrine of Our Lady; Janów Podlaski – Poland's oldest and most famous stud farm, producing purebred Arabs (the venue of a large auction held each August).

THE BIEBRZA VALLEY

The Biebrza is a northern tributary of the Narew. Its valley, surrounded by morainic hills, occupies an area of ca. 250,000 hectares, of which 100,000 hectares is a peat bog. This is the only marshland area of this size left in Central Europe – a pristine environment hostile to man, but invariably beautiful. In springtime, when meltwater fills the entire valley with extensive seasonal lakes, man feels an intruder in this enormous waterfowl sanctuary. The only usable means of transport at this time of year is a flat-bottomed boat or a canoe. The vast expanse of the marshes can be better appreciated from one of the high observation towers that have been put up for the benefit of the tourists. However, the landscape is far from monotonous.

A variety of environments coexist in the Biebrza valley: raised bogs in the desolate and inaccessible Czerwone Bagno ("Red Swamp"), sandy desert in an area called Grzędy, and blanket bogs in Bagno Podlaskie ("Podlasie Swamp") – it is small wonder then that the region has been entered onto the list of World Biosphere Reserves. Those hard-to-reach marshlands, waterlogged meadows and peat bogs are now protected, as they fall within the Biebrza National Park. There are 235 bird species living on the river, including 29 vanishing species (among others, the white-tailed eagle, the hawk, and the ruff), as well as a sizeable beaver population. Other animals inhabiting the National Park include the elk, deer, roe deer, wolf, fox, racoon dog, badger and ermine.

This is a region where nature can still be stronger than technology. At the edge of the marshland, near the confluence of the Biebrza and Narew, a hill named Strękowa Góra rises above the valley. From 8 to 10 September 1939, a small infantry detachment under the command of Captain Władysław Raginis, kept in check from its fortified hilltop position the prevailing forces of the German 19th Armoured Corps – General Guderian's tanks were unable to bypass the Polish outpost through the swamp. Having run out of munitions, with most of his men dead, Captain Raginis took his own life, blowing up the fort.

1. The "Red Swamp" in the Biebrza Valley.
2. A delicate cobweb.
3. The Biebrza flood plains near Goniądz in springtime.

➡ Open-air museum of folk architecture from the Kurpie region; Szczuczyn – a formerly Piarist monastery complex from the turn of the 17th cent. with the Baroque Church of St. Mary.

THE AUGUSTÓW CANAL

The Biebrza and Narew are connected with the Neman by means of the Augustów Canal – a historic monument that surpasses all others in terms of length! Navigable for vessels of up to 100 tons, the 102-kilometre-long canal cuts through the Suwałki Lakeland, joining the river systems of the Vistula and the Neman. In view of the considerable difference in elevation between the starting and end points, there are 18 locks on the way. The channel was designed by General Ignacy Prądzynski, who also supervised its construction in 1824-1839. Today, it is used for timber floating and pleasure cruises. Itself an interesting monument of 19th-century technology, the canal traverses the majestic Augustów Forest – the land of the mysterious Jatzvingian tribe.

The forest is named after the town of Augustów, founded in 1546. Situated partly in the Suwałki Lakeland and partly in the Augustów Plain, the forest covers a total area (within Polish borders) of 114,000 hectares. It was not until the 16th century that the first settlers arrived here and trade in timber and its derivatives (tar, potash etc.) began. Coniferous trees predominate in the forest, and the local flora includes several relict plants from the post-glacial era. More than 10 nature reserves have been established, mostly for the protection of the forest's biocenoses. Numerous lakes and rivers (e.g. the Czarna Hańcza and Rozpuda) add to the beauty of the landscape. The entire Suwałki Lakeland is characterised by varied landforms (with morainic hills of up to 300 metres above sea level). Trough lakes abound in the region, one of which – Lake Hańcza – is the deepest in Central European Plain (108.5 metres). The other common type of lake is the thaw lake, such is Lake Wigry.

But this idyllic region has its tragic history, too. In the village of Giby, there is a deeply moving memorial to the victims of the Soviet NKVD – a pile of rocks, each symbolising a killed or missing person. Cultural landmarks were not left untouched, either. For instance, the magnificent Neo-Gothic palace at Dowspuda, the property of Ludwik Michał Pac, has not survived to the present day.

1. The Augustów Canal.
2. The monastery on Lake Wigry.

➡ Wigry – a Baroque Camaldolese complex, comprising the Church of the Immaculate Conception (1704–1745), hermits' lodges (17th-18th cent.) and a 17th-cent. clock tower.

LAKELANDS AND THE COAST

To the west of the Suwałki Lakeland lie the Great Masurian Lakes. In the early Middle Ages, Masuria was inhabited by the Baltic Prussian tribe, and from the 13th century on, it was under the rule of the Teutonic Knights. After the Treaty of Toruń of 1466, it became a Polish fief – East Prussia (from 1525 – Ducal Prussia). In the 14th-17th centuries, this land was colonised by settlers from Mazovia and, consequently, Polonised. After the Partitions of Poland, Germanisation began, as a result of which Poland lost the plebiscite held in the province in 1920, as it did in nearby Warmia. The latter territory borders on the west on Żuławy, or Vistula Fens, on the beautiful Kaszuby, and on the wooded Bory Tucholskie region.

A little further to the west extends yet another historic region – Pomerania. For centuries, it was the scene of rivalry between Polish and German ethnic groups, the latter represented, in turn, by Brandenburg, the Teutonic Order and the Kingdom of Prussia. In the 11th century, a local dynasty emerged in Eastern Pomerania, which in 1138 became part of Poland. In 1308, Eastern Pomerania was incorporated into the Teutonic State; recaptured in the following century, it became the Polish province of "Royal Prussia". In Western Pomerania, the local dynasty held on. However, in 1181, Duke Bogusław I submitted to the Holy Roman Empire. In 1185–1227, Western Pomerania found itself under Danish rule, but afterwards returned to Poland. The strongest links with Poland were maintained by the province of Słupsk. After 1637, Western Pomerania remained first under Swedish and then Prussian rule.

Pomerania is a very scenic land, with broad, sandy beaches, high cliffs and shallow coastal lakes. There are places still to be found where the landscape has not changed since the Middle Ages, despite increasing tourist traffic, industrial development and urbanisation. The Baltic itself – a shallow inland sea – forms Poland's northern border along a distance of about 500 kilometres.

1. The Ostróda-Elbląg Canal in the Masurian Lakeland.
2. A fishing port.

GREAT MASURIAN LAKES

The Masurian Lakeland is an enchanting area. The tranquil lakes, dense woodland of the Pisz Forest, clean air, and abundance and diversity of historic monuments – all this makes the region one of Poland's most popular holiday destinations. Niegocin, Mamry, Śniardwy, Jeziorak and hundreds of other lakes attract nature lovers, sailing enthusiasts, mushroompickers, hunters and bird-watchers. This is also the angler's paradise, as the lakes are home to many species of fish, including the mighty pike. For ages, the *Mazury* versus *Ost Preussen* controversy was a bone of contention between the Poles and the Germans. Both parties to the dispute tried to curry favour with the indigenous population. Today, the rivalry has subsided and it is high time to take care of the abandoned *Junker* palaces, forgotten amid neglected parks. After all, we do take care of Polish relics in the former Polish borderlands. Masuria is one of the "small motherlands", the common heritage of several nations, which should unite, and not divide people – as they are united by the landmarks of the past that reflect the difficult history of the region.

Święta Lipka, near the lakeside resort of Mrągowo, is a famous pilgrimage destination. The Baroque monastery complex is dominated by the Church of the Visitation, built in 1688–1693 by the architect Jerzy Ertli from Vilnius. The church, housing a miraculous painting of the Virgin (crowned in 1968) is one of the highlights of Polish Baroque architecture. Inside, the rich decoration is supplemented with *trompe l'oeil* murals by Maciej Jan Mayer. The church has a beautiful, Baroque organ, built in Königsberg in the 18th century, with an Annunciation scene played out by mechanised figures. This is a very old place of Marian cult: in the 12th century, so the legend goes, St. Mary appeared miraculously in an old linden tree (hence the name Święta Lipka – "Holy Linden"). The trunk of that tree can now be seen in the church in front of the pulpit, supporting a silver figure of the Virgin. For centuries, the place has been visited by hosts of pilgrims, including kings of Poland: Zygmunt III, Władysław IV, Jan Kazimierz and Jan III Sobieski.

1. Lake Mokre.
2. The Święta Lipka shrine.

➡ Sejny – the former Dominican monastery and basilica of the Visitation (17th-18th cent.); a retable with a figure of St. Mary in one of the basilica's chapels; the Massalski chapel from 1666.

LIDZBARK WARMIŃSKI

Lidzbark Warmiński, the capital of the Warmia region, was originally called Lecbarg and was an important settlement of the pagan Prussians. Formally, it was incorporated into the estate of the Bishop of Warmia in the mid-13th century, but the Prussians held it until the end of the uprising of 1273. The bishopric, established in 1243 in Braniewo, was subsequently moved to Orneta and, finally, to Lidzbark. The position of the Warmian Bishops differed from that of other hierarchs: they combined their ecclesiastical function with the role of administrators of the province.

In the 15th century, the towns and nobility of Warmia, tired of Teutonic rule, formed the Prussian League and appealed to the King of Poland for protection. Under the terms of the Second Treaty of Toruń, which concluded the ensuing Thirteen Years' War in 1466, Warmia was incorporated into Poland as an enclave linked with "Royal Prussia" by only a narrow strip of land near Elbląg. Among the Warmian Bishops who resided in Lidzbark were Jan Dantyszek, Marcin Kromer and Ignacy Krasicki. In the local library, Adam Grabowski found, in 1749, the Gallus Anonimus *Chronicle* from the early 12th century.

Lidzbark Castle ranks among the most splendid medieval residences in Poland. It occupies the upper part of a high ground at the confluence of the Łyna and Symsarna Rivers, while the rest of the escarpment is a forecourt, delimited by a moat. Construction of the castle was undertaken by Bishop Jan of Meissen (1350–1355) and its main parts were completed by Henryk III (1373–1401). Stern and a little gloomy on the outside, the castle reveals a striking variety of form inside. It has a picturesque courtyard, surrounded by two tiers of arcades supported on granite pillars. The most interesting interiors include the Great Refectory and the castle chapel decorated with excellent woodcarving. Preserved Gothic murals are found in most of the chambers and in the arcades. Under Prussian rule, the castle was used as a barracks, a military hospital and a storehouse. These days it houses the Museum of Warmia, with exhibitions of late Gothic art, furniture, handicraft and 20th century Polish painting.

1. The Great Refectory in the castle.
2. The Bishops' Castle at Lidzbark Warmiński.

➡ Gierłoż – Hitler's headquarters known as the "Wolf's Lair" (*Wolfsschanze*), the site of an abortive attempt on the Führer's life on 22 July 1944; Olsztynek – open-air museum of Masurian folk architecture.

TORUŃ

Toruń is one of Poland's most beautiful towns. It has retained much of its medieval atmosphere and has been included in UNESCO's World Heritage List. In 1236, a castle of the Teutonic Knights replaced the old fortified settlement on the Vistula, becoming the first Teutonic stronghold on Polish territory. In 1454, the Toruń burghers rebelled against the Knights, and the peace settlement after the ensuing war returned the town to Poland in 1466. Toruń was a Hanseatic town, had the right to mint its own coinage, and was considered to be one of the richest towns in Poland; it was also a bastion of Protestantism. The medieval town plan has been preserved till this day, as has the town hall, built by Master Andrzej in 1393 – one of the finest examples of municipal architecture in Europe. In 1602–1605, the building was heightened and decorated with Mannerist gables and turrets, designed by a Flemish architect from Gdańsk, Antonius van Opbergen.

The dominant accents in the town's skyline are the Old Town parish church and the Church of SS. John the Baptist and John the Evangelist – a Gothic hall built between 1270 and 1330 and enlarged in the 15th century, with rich decoration and furnishings from the 14th-18th centuries (e.g., the St. Wolfgang Triptych from ca. 1502–1506 and the brass epitaph of Mayor Jan von Soest and his wife from ca. 1360). Its splendour is matched by the Gothic Church of Our Lady, raised in the 13th century, and subsequently enlarged in 1350–1370 to form an aisled hall. Between 1557 and 1724, it was used by the Protestant community. The parish church of the New Town district was dedicated to St. James; it was a Gothic basilica built by the Teutonic Knights in 1309–1350, with an elongated chancel and a row of chapels on either side of the corpus. The highlight of the church is the mystical and expressive Christ Crucified upon the Tree of Life from the late 14th century. There are many historic residential houses in Toruń as well, dating back to the 14th-18th centuries. Tall and narrow Gothic houses (e.g. the Copernicus House) contrast with the Mannerist and Baroque gables (e.g. in the "Star House" façade of 1697). Partly preserved monuments include the ruins of the Teutonic castle, some sections of the city walls with gates and towers, as well as several Gothic granaries.

1. The Gothic Town Hall in Toruń's Market Square.
2. View of the town from across the Vistula.

➡ Arsenal from 1824; Prussian fortifications from 1818-1914, Baroque palaces, residential buildings with Art Nouveau decorations from ca. 1900, as well as public buildings from the inter-war period.

PELPLIN

Of all the Cistercian abbeys in Pomerania, the one in Pelplin was the largest and most splendid. The Cistercians had been invited to Pomerania by Duke Sambor II. His successor, Mestwin II, endowed them in 1274 with the village of Pelplin, in which they built an abbey within a couple of years. The first church at the site was erected around 1320, and was considerably enlarged towards the end of the century. When the work was completed in ca. 1400, all that was left of the former monastic buildings was the old oratory, subsequently used as the chapter house. In the centuries to follow, the complex was further enlarged, so now it constitutes a record of the changing fashions and styles in Pomeranian architecture. The church is a large hall (84 metres long) with an enormous transept. Its dimensions provide a striking contrast with the one-storey houses in the village. On the outside, the appearance of the building is not too exciting, perhaps with the exception of the north portal, lavishly adorned with floral motifs and figures of saints and angels. Above is a tympanum with a figure of Christ preaching. The interior, by contrast, is extremely rich and may even seem overloaded with altars, gilt ornaments, murals and sculptures. The high altar is a six-tier structure, 25-metre high – one of the largest and most magnificent retables in Poland. Built in 1623–1624, it holds a painting by Hermann Hahn of the Coronation of Our Lady. The mid-15th century stalls are noted for their elaborate decoration. Adjoining the church is a large, square-shaped Gothic cloister, with Gothic murals and Baroque paintings – among these, works by Bartholomäus Strobel. In 1823, the Prussian authorities dissolved the Cistercian order, so a new use had to be found for the imposing Pelplin church. It was accordingly raised to the rank of cathedral church of the Chełmno Diocese, which was then much larger than it is today. The Diocesan Museum houses a huge collection of valuable exhibits, including Gothic sculpture and liturgical vestments. But unquestionable pride of place goes to a copy of Johann Gutenberg's Bible from 1453.

1. *Pelplin Cathedral.*
2. *North portal with a tympanum.*
3. *Cathedral interior.*

➡ Tczew – the Vistula Museum devoted to the role of the "Queen of Polish Rivers" in history; Gorzędziej – St. Adalbert's Church built on the site of a 10th-cent. fortified settlement.

FROMBORK

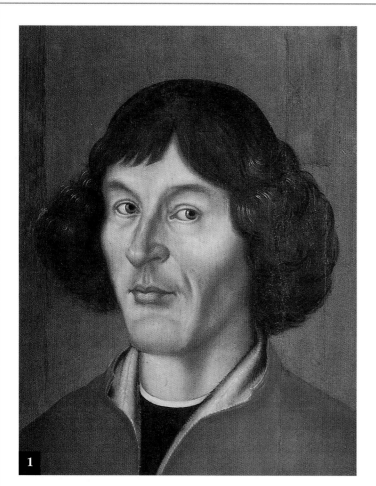

The cathedral and bishops' residence towering above the Vistula Bay stand on the edge of the Elbląg Plateau, whose rim descends steeply towards the water. Initially, it was the site of a pagan settlement, replaced by a provisional stronghold of the Teutonic Knights, or, perhaps, a bishop's fortified residence. Between 1261 and 1278, Frombork became the seat of the Chapter of Warmia and of the cathedral (previously located at Braniewo). The cathedral, whose construction began in 1330, was consecrated in 1342. Its interior is richly furnished, the highlight being the magnificent organ – the work of the Gdańsk workshop of Daniel Nitrowski from 1683–1686. The church is surrounded with a complex of buildings and fortifications. Their southwestern corner is protected by a polygonal artillery tower with a belfry added on top. In the late Middle Ages, the fortified cathedral complex was repeatedly besieged and captured by Polish, Teutonic and Bohemian forces. An august tower today bears the name of Nicolaus Copernicus, although the famous astronomer (whose epitaph is in the cathedral) in actual fact carried out his observations of heavenly bodies elsewhere – from a canons' house, outside the fortifications' perimeter.

Copernicus (1473–1543), the inventor of the heliocentric model of the universe, was the greatest Renaissance mind in Poland. In 1510, he settled in Frombork as a canon of the Warmian Chapter. It was here that he made his observations and wrote his magnum opus – *De Revolutionibus Orbium Coelestium* ("On the rotations of the heavenly bodies"). His theory struck at the very foundations of established views on the structure of the universe and met with a hostile reception from both the academic world and the church. Even so, from the turn of the 16th century, the theory began to gain more and more adherents. Its ultimate acceptance was largely due to the work of Johannes Kepler and Galileo. However, it was not until 1833 that Copernicus' treatise was taken off the index of prohibited books. The Copernican Museum in the former Bishops' Palace presents an extensive exhibition devoted to the man's life and work.

1. Nicolaus Copernicus.
2. Cathedral Hill in Frombork.

➜ Krynica Morska - beautiful seaside resort on the Bay of Gdańsk; Braniewo, Morąg, Orneta and Pasłek - mediaeval towns with a preserved urban plan, old houses, magnificent churches and city walls.

MALBORK

Malbork Castle, once the seat of the Grand Master of the Order of the Hospital of St. Mary in Jerusalem (more widely known under the name of the "Teutonic Knights") is one of the largest castles in Europe. Its construction began in 1274 on the initiative of Theodoric Gatirslebe and Hermann von Schönenberg. In 1309, Malbork became the capital of the Teutonic State, but the Grand Master himself settled there only in 1324. Enlarged in the 14th century, Malbork was considered to be impregnable. Indeed, King Władysław Jagiełło, after the victory at Grunwald in 1410, failed to capture Malbork. In order to accomplish this feat half a century later, his son Kazimierz resorted to bribing mercenaries in the service of the Teutonic Knights. Following the Treaty of Toruń (1466), Malbork was incorporated into Poland and for several centuries remained the seat of a Crown *starostwo* and one of the largest national arsenals.

This formidable Gothic stronghold consists of three parts: the High Castle (1276–1280, remodelled in 1331–1344), the Middle Castle with the Great Refectory (1318–1324) and Grand Master's Palace (1383–1399), and the Outer Castle (14th century). In 1331–1344, a new church was put up at the castle – 38 metres long and 14.4 metres high. The chancel, protruding from the outer face of the walls, had a triangular crowning with a huge, 7-metre high, outward-facing figure of the Blessed Virgin Mary – the patron saint of the Teutonic Order (destroyed in 1945). The High Castle is a typical monastic castle on a quadrangular plan with an inner courtyard. The most interesting part of the Middle Castle is the Great Refectory. Another architectural gem is the Grand Master's Palace - which occupies the outer end of the castle's western wing. This is a most elegant residence, in which concern for prestige seems to take precedence over defence considerations. After the First Partition of Poland in 1772, the castle was transformed into a Prussian barracks and fell into disrepair. Painstakingly restored in 1882–1921, it was subsequently damaged during the Soviet offensive in 1945. Nowadays, the castle houses a museum and has been entered onto UNESCO's World Heritage List.

1. The Teutonic Knights' Castle at Malbork.
2. Portal with the Wise and Foolish Virgins.

➡ Elbląg – totally destroyed during the Second World War, it was rebuilt, and its original urban layout has recently been recreated; the 19th-cent. Elbląg Canal.

Teutonic Castles

The Teutonic Knights evolved out of a German hospital fraternity established near Acre in 1190, during the Third Crusade. In 1198, the fraternity was transformed into a chivalric order, the principal tasks of which included warring with unbelievers. The knights wore characteristic white mantles with a black cross at the left-hand side (hence their Polish name *Krzyżacy*, or "Knights of the Cross"). In 1226, the Teutonic Knights were approached by Prince Konrad of Mazovia, who invested them with the province of Chełmno in exchange for protection against pagan Baltic tribes. That land became the nucleus of the future Teutonic State, the formation of which spelled centuries of trouble for Poland on her northern flank in Prussia, Warmia and Pomerania. Polish-Teutonic relations consisted of a string of wars, broken treaties, treacherous acts and mutual accusations. But leaving emotions aside, Teutonic rule did bring about progress in those territories through the introduction of new forms of state organisation, efficient management, and – most importantly – through knowledge of modern warfare and the ways of building impregnable fortresses.

Kwidzyn Castle, in the province formerly known as Pomezania, has the typical features of a Teutonic castle. The town of Kwidzyn was founded by the Teutonic Knights in 1233. The Gothic complex, built in the 14th century on a square plan, comprised the castle and the cathedral. One of its most conspicuous features is the enormous dansker tower, overhanging beyond the line of walls. From today's perspective, it seems hard to believe that this enormous structure served mainly as the castle latrine. The town of Golub was the property of the Kujawy bishops, but in 1293 it passed into the hands of the Teutonic Knights. In the early 14th century, Komtur Conrad Sack built a Gothic castle there, captured in 1410 and 1422 by the Polish army. Remodelled and decorated with a Mannerist parapet in 1611–1625, it was the residence of Anna Vasa. Today, it is a place where, in deference to tradition, mock jousting tournaments are held. Further to the West, in Kashubia, lies the town of Bytów with a Gothic castle, remodelled in the 16th-17th centuries by the Pomeranian Dukes. Today, the castle is the seat of the Western Kashubia Museum.

1. Kwidzyn Castle.
2. Jousting tournament at Golub-Dobrzyń.
3. Bytów Castle.

➔ Reszel, Barciany, Ostróda, Szczytno, Nidzica, Gniew, Sztum and other towns – imposing castles of the Teutonic Knights, showing considerable variation due to divergent historical development.

ŻUŁAWY

Until the 13th, the region of Żuławy – today forming a fragment of the East Pomeranian coastal area – literally did not exist: it was almost totally submerged in the Baltic Sea. This is an area where the Vistula, building up a delta from the debris carried by its waters, has been contending with the sea. In the 14th century, the Teutonic Knights ordered the construction of dikes, dams and drainage canals, drawing freely on Dutch models. The polders thus reclaimed, situated in a depression, had extraordinarily fertile soil, which attracted large-scale Dutch and German settlement. The subsequent history of Żuławy was similar to that of other lands held by the Teutonic Knights, and in 1466 the region was incorporated into Poland. In 1945, it was flooded when the dams were blown up. It was one of the last pockets of resistance of the German troops, who held their positions until 9 May. The reclamation and recultivation of the area took several years. The landscape here is flat and slightly monotonous, but the views of the fields, canals, rows of willows and windmills do indeed have a certain charm. Such scenery provides an excellent backdrop for the Gothic village churches and the timber cottages where the Dutch settlers used to live.

To the West, Żuławy merges imperceptibly with Kashubia – another region, besides Podhale, where folk tradition and culture are still very much alive and fairly authentic. The Kashubians are the indigenous population of Eastern Pomerania, with their own dialect, literature and folklore, and a strong attachment to the Catholic tradition. The hallmarks of Kashubian handicraft are embroidery, painted furniture, earthenware and snuff-boxes made of horn. To learn more about Kashubian folk culture, worthwhile trips can be made to the Kaszuby Museum in Kartuzy or the open-air museum at Wdzydze Kiszewskie. The entire region is highly attractive for tourists, especially for water sports enthusiasts. There are also interesting local legends about giants and other supernatural beings, one of whom – Smętek – is said to embody the spirit of Kashubia, so distinctly perceptible on the Żuławy polders, among the lakeland woods of Szwajcaria Kaszubska or on the morainic height of Kępa Redłowska, overlooking the Baltic.

1. Oxbow lake at Drewnica.
2. Low-lying polder in the Vistula delta.
3. The Żuławy landscape.

➡ Szwajcaria Kaszubska – a scenic land of hills, 400 lakes and forests.

GDAŃSK

Gdańsk – once an important centre of European commerce – has an inimitable atmosphere of its own which combines the freedom of a harbour town with the dignity of an age-old cultural centre. This may also be due to the openness and tolerance of the merchant community on which the town's prosperity was founded. Gdańsk has been regarded as the capital of the Kashubians, as a German town, as a Polish town – and all these statements are simultaneously true (not to forget about the contribution of the Dutch, Scots and Livonians to its development!).

Gdańsk has held its municipal charter since 1236, but only in the 14th century did it begin to thrive. In 1440, it joined the Prussian League and in 1454 became incorporated into Poland. As part of the Polish state, Gdańsk enjoyed a considerable measure of autonomy. On several occasions, the city's commercial interests clashed with the political line followed by the Polish monarchy, which was thus forced to take appropriate action. In 1807–1815, Gdańsk was a free city. The 19th century brought a new phase of development connected with the enlargement of the harbour and the construction of railway lines. After the First World War, Gdańsk once again became a free city. On 1 September 1939, the German attack on the Westerplatte fort and the Polish post office in Gdańsk marked the outbreak of the Second World War. German rule in Gdańsk ended in 1945, when the city was captured by the Red Army. Once the front had moved on, Gdańsk was looted and destroyed in a barbarous fashion. The burnt-out ruins were ceded to Poland at the Potsdam Conference after the war. In the 1950s and 1960s, a massive reconstruction effort was undertaken and successfully completed.

In our times, Gdańsk was once again a scene of historic events. On 31 August 1980, an agreement was signed at Gdańsk Shipyard between the striking workers and the government, which paved the way for the formation of "Solidarity", led by Lech Wałęsa, the future president of Poland. It was a move which – along with the election of Pope John Paul II – started the avalanche that ultimately swept the Berlin Wall out of existence and put an end to Communist rule in Central Europe.

1. Panorama of Gdańsk.
2. August 1980: Lech Wałęsa with a copy of the Gdańsk Agreement.

➡ Monument to the victims of the 1970 riots – three symbolic crosses at the entrance to the shipyard; Westerplatte – the place where the Second World War began.

The backbone of historic Gdańsk is the so-called "Main Town", following the axis of Długa Street, which broadens into Długi Targ ("Long Market"). The entire urban plan of the Main Town is itself a historic monument of the highest rank. The principal places of interest in this part of Gdańsk include: St. Mary's Church (15th c.), St. John's church (15th c.), the Dominican Church (14th c.) with Baroque and Rococo decoration, the late Gothic Court of The Fraternity of St. George (15th c.), and several residential houses (15th-18th c.) with Mannerist façades. Also worth noting are the city fortifications: walls with towers (14th c.), the Gothic Prison Tower (15th c.), the Mannerist High Gate (16th c.), the Golden Gate (17th c.) and the Grand Arsenal (17th c.).

Długa Street, and especially Długi Targ, lie at the very heart of the city; they also boast the most splendid burgher houses and municipal buildings. At the corner of Długi Targ is the Town Hall with preserved and carefully refurbished interiors. This late Gothic structure was built in stages (1379–1382, before 1462 and 1489–1492), gaining in height and acquiring a slender tower with a lofty spire, crowned with a figure of King Zygmunt August. Inside, the Town Hall is Flemish Mannerism at its best. The opulence and, to some extent, extravagance of the citizens of old Gdańsk are evidenced by the Great Council Chamber, also called the Red Hall after the velvet covering of the walls. It was designed by Hans Vredeman de Vries, whose allegorical paintings adorn the walls, decorated with woodcarving and inlays by Simon Herle. The ceiling boasts several magnificent paintings.

Another municipal building worth seeing is the Guild Hall (known as "Artus Court"). There are also a number of burgher houses that merit a closer look, including the "Royal House" (Kamienica Królewska), whose entire façade is decorated in sculpture. The most ancient part of Gdańsk – the Old Town, divided by the Radunia Canal – is situated to the north of the Main Town. All the districts of Gdańsk abound in invaluable historical monuments.

1. Great Council Chamber in the Town Hall.
2. Długi Targ – the heart of Gdańsk.

➡ St. Catherine's – a 14th-cent. hall church (epitaph of the 17th-cent. astronomer Johannes Hevelius) and the adjacent Preachers' House.

GDAŃSK

Gdańsk's livelihood depended on the Vistula and sea trade. It is thus small wonder that the most prestigious of the city's squares was decorated in 1615 with a fountain sporting a figure of Neptune. The sea god protected the sailors, who passed through the Green Gate (the official Gdańsk residence of the kings of Poland) to the Long Wharf to board their ships bound for Riga, Amsterdam, or the distant ports of Spain. The main port was located on the Motława River, and across the river, on Granary Island, were the warehouses where Polish grain exported to Western Europe was stored. The ships brought back luxurious goods, bought on the spot by the gentry, who flocked to the city in great numbers. Thus, almost all the money received for grain would immediately return to the coffers of Gdańsk's merchants.

As regards its architecture, 16th- and 17th-century Gdańsk could easily match the royal Cracow. The Renaissance burgher houses from that period have decorative triangular gables and fine sculptural decoration on the window and door surrounds. The most beautiful of these is the Golden House, which owes its name to the gilded bas-reliefs covering the façade. Contrary to rumours that it was brought over to Gdańsk in pieces from faraway lands, it was actually built right where it stands in the early 17th century.

Parallel to Długi Targ runs Mariacka Street, where the houses are fronted with characteristic terraces, raised slightly above street level, with decorative railings or balustrades. Today, many of these buildings house shops selling items made from "Baltic gold" – amber. Taking the obligatory walk along the Motława, the tourists pass along the city's fortifications (including the Green Gate, Breadsellers' Gate and St. Mary's Gate) to reach the Great Crane – a unique combination of a gate, tower and harbour crane. This 15th-century structure is now part of the fascinating Maritime Museum.

1. The medieval Żuraw, or Great Crane, on the waterfront.
2. Terraces in Mariacka Street.

➡ Gdynia – sea harbour, museum-ships (*Błyskawica* – a destroyer, and *Dar Pomorza* – a three-masted frigate), Oceanographic Museum, Marine Aquarium.

The affluence of old Gdańsk can be seen in the Gothic Church of St. Mary. It is the largest church in Poland (105 metres long) – an aisled hall with a transept (66 metres wide) and square tower (78 metres high) – and the world's largest brick church, with a cubic capacity equal to that of St. Vitus in Vienna and Notre Dame in Paris. Previous churches on this site were far more modest. A basilica, whose construction began in 1343, already in 1379 turned out to be too small to satisfy the ambition of the local oligarchy, who accordingly commissioned Heinrich Ungeradin to build a new one. The task took long to complete. By 1447, only the eastern part of the church with the aisled chancel and transept had been built; in 1484–1496 the corpus was added, with the vaults going up in 1499–1502. Upon completion, the church could hold a congregation of twenty-five thousand!

The interior of St. Mary's used to be a real museum of treasures (with more than ten Gothic altarpieces and a great number of funerary monuments and epitaphs, paintings, sculptures etc.). Tragically, the church burnt down in 1945 and what can be seen today is the result of restoration. The high altar – an immense Gothic-Renaissance polyptych (1511–1517) from the workshop of Master Michael of Augsburg – was badly damaged in 1945, too, and is in part a reconstruction.

The austere church interior with exquisite vaulting (star, net and cellular), supported on 26 pillars, houses several valuable works of art, including a 15th-century "Beautiful Madonna", an impressive Passion group on the enormous rood beam, and a copy of *The Last Judgement* by Hans Memling (the original can be seen in the National Museum). Originally commissioned by a Genoese banker, the triptych was captured by a Gdańsk privateer, who then offered his loot to the church in his home town.

Next to St. Mary's is the Baroque Royal Chapel, built in 1678–1681 by Tylman van Gameren, and a Gothic vicarage dating back to 1518.

1. St. Mary's interior.
2. The Last Judgement *by Hans Memling*.
3. Portrait of the Young Gabriel Schumann *by Andreas Stech*.

➡ National Museum in the former Franciscan monastery, featuring Polish and foreign painting, Gdańsk furniture and Gothic sculpture, as well as a treasury with precious gold- and silverware.

GDAŃSK-OLIWA

A Kashubian hymn ends with the declaration: "We side with God." This is indeed confirmed by the abundance of churches in the region. Alongside the brick and half-timbered churches in East Pomerania, there are immense monastic foundations.

The most famous monastery is at Oliwa. Now a district of Gdańsk, it was originally a settlement clustered around the Cistercian abbey founded in ca. 1186 by the Pomeranian Duke Sambor I, who installed there monks from Kołbacz. In the first stage, a Romanesque-Gothic chancel and transept were constructed in the 13th century. In the 14th century, the church was enlarged, assuming an extremely elongated shape (107 metres long). This Gothic cathedral with a Rococo façade from 1771 is richly furnished. The paintings by Bartholomäus Strobel, Hermann Hahn and A. Tech provide a fitting background for the Renaissance stalls and the famous Rococo organ, the work of Jan Wulff from Orneta (built in 1763–1788), deservedly praised by musicians and music lovers. Since 1958, International Organ Music Festivals have been regularly held at Oliwa. The Oliwa church became a cathedral upon the dissolution of the monastery, when the magnificent church building was given to the Gdańsk diocese.

The church is surrounded with former monastic buildings. Of special interest are the chapter house, with a vault supported on stone pillars, and the Great Refectory. The old monastery is now the seat of the Diocesan Museum. Situated in Oliwa Park (a formal garden set up ca. 1760 to the design of Kazimierz Dębiński, with a valuable rockery and botanical garden) is the mid-18th-century Rococo Abbots' Palace (with a 15th-century east wing).

Oliwa is the northernmost of Poland's "grand monuments". This is not to say that there is nothing to see further north. Far from it. The Bay of Gdańsk coast is dotted with beautiful holiday resorts and charming old towns.

Not to be missed are the 19th-century resort of Sopot and the fishing ports and churches at Puck and Władysławowo. And having got thus far, it would be a pity to miss the clean, sandy beaches of Jastrzębia Góra, from which a walk can be taken to the northernmost point in Poland – Cape Rozewie with an old lighthouse.

1. Oliwa Cathedral.
2. Fishing boats at Kuźnica Morska.

➡ Wejherowo – 26 Calvary chapels founded in 1649 by Jakub Wejher, one of the pilgrimage sites of the Kashubians; 17th-cent. Reformati Church.

ŁEBA

The Baltic coast may not be the ideal place for a seaside holiday. The weather can be changeable and windy, and the sea is not always as clean as one might wish. Having said that, it is nevertheless an extremely attractive tourist area. Broad, sandy beaches alternate with steep cliffs; there are coastal lakes populated with rare species of water fowl; and the wooded dunes offer peace and privacy that is hard to find at the most famous beaches on the Mediterranean.

The small town of Hel, at the tip of the eponymous peninsula, was granted a municipal charter in 1378. Fishing has always been the mainstay of the town's economy. In 1939, it was one of the last points of resistance in Poland to capitulate to the German invaders: the local garrison held out until 2 October. After the war, Hel remained for 40 years a military zone closed to visitors. Things to be seen there include the 14th-century Gothic church (now a Fisheries Museum), an 18th-century half-timbered inn, old fishermen's houses, and interesting fortifications from the years preceding the Second World War. A string of seaside resorts extends westwards of Hel, the best-known being Jurata, Cetniewo, Jastrzębia Góra and Karwia.

Łeba, a little further to the west, is a resort renowned for its broad and clean beaches. This old Kashubian settlement, situated between Lake Łebsko and Lake Sarbsko, received its charter in 1357. However, the combined threat of the sea, constantly eating at the coast, and the shifting sand dunes, necessitated its relocation further inland in 1570. Remnants of a 14th-century church have survived among the dunes. Some of the dunes on the isthmus between the sea coast and Lake Łebsko attain a height of ca. 50 metres. This area is part of the Słowiński National Park, declared a World Biosphere Reserve in 1977. On the marshlands to the south of Łeba and at Bielawskie Błota, relic Atlantic and tundra vegetation has survived. In the nearby village of Kluki, there is an open-air museum exhibiting cottages of the Slovincians – a Slavonic ethnic group which became Germanised an practically disappeared in the first half of the 20th century.

1. Łeba – the shifting dunes.
2. Sandy beaches on the Baltic coast.

➡ Hel, Rozewie, Niechorze, Kołobrzeg and Gąski – the best-known lighthouses on the Baltic coast (most of them can be climbed, the magnificent views amply rewarding the effort).

TRZĘSACZ

The old coastal towns of Kołobrzeg, Darłowo and Ustka give the tourist a foretaste of other interesting places further inland, noted either for their pristine natural beauty, or for their historic monuments – such as at Wejherowo, Lębork, Sławno and Koszalin. This region saw much heavy fighting towards the end of the Second World War, particularly at Kołobrzeg. Regrettably, most of the old towns shared the fate of Gdańsk – they either burnt down during the hostilities, or were deliberately reduced to rubble afterwards. At some places, the historic districts were never reconstructed, the bricks being used instead for the reconstruction of Warsaw's Old Town.

Kołobrzeg is a port town at the mouth of the Parsęta. A settlement, one of the oldest in Pomerania, existed there already in the 7th-8th centuries. The inhabitants made a living from salt production and trade. A bishopric was established as early as AD 1000, and in 1255 Kołobrzeg received its municipal charter. In the mid-19th century, this former Hanseatic town gained the reputation of a spa and seaside resort. In 1945, nearly 90% of it was destroyed during the attack of the Polish 1st Army on fortified German positions.

The town of Słupsk was luckier, with a number of historic buildings escaping destruction: the Gothic parish church from the 14th cent., the 15th-cent. former Dominican Church, the 15th-cent. Premonstratensian Church, the 15th-cent. city walls with two gates and the Witches' Tower (15th cent.). The Gothic Castle built in the 16th century by Duke Bogusław X – the seat of the Dukes of Słupsk and Pomerania – was converted by Frederick William I into a barracks in the 18th century. Near the castle is an old mill – one of Poland's earliest monuments of industrial architecture.

Pomeranian towns had their vicissitudes, but in the end always managed to survive. Trzęsacz, however, did not. Situated at the edge of a cliff, it was gradually taken away by the sea. The inhabitants had to go, leaving behind their houses, which have long since been submerged under water. In time, the village church also collapsed. A solitary southern wall perched on the cliff is all that remains of this once-proud Gothic edifice. And one day it, too, will be claimed by the waves.

1. Ruins of the church at Trzęsacz.
2. Cliff on Wolin Island.

➡ Trzebiatów – 15th-cent. Gothic church, 15th-cent. late Gothic chapels, remnants of 13th-cent. city walls, 15th-cent. town hall; narrow-gauge railway connecting Trzebiatów with Gryfice.

KAMIEŃ POMORSKI

On the bank of Kamień Bay, which separates Wolin Island from the mainland, lies the captivating little town of Kamień Pomorski. In the 9th-11th centuries, it was a fortified settlement inhabited mainly by fishermen, in the 12th century becoming a ducal seat. In subsequent years, it further grew in importance as a bishopric and a major port. In 1274, Kamień was granted a municipal charter and in the following century joined the Hanseatic League. Mineral waters, discovered in the mid-19th century, account for the town's status of a health resort.

The monuments to be seen include the Bishops' Palace (16th c.), fragments of the city walls (13th-14th c.), the town hall (15th-16th c., burnt in 1945), and the Romanesque-Gothic cathedral. Its construction began towards the end of the 13th century, first in stone and then in brick, and it is the oldest structure in Poland utilising this latter, previously unknown material. In 1273 and 1308, Kamień was invaded by Brandenburgers, who damaged the cathedral. It was accordingly restored and remodelled in the late 14th century. The monumental interior is richly furnished, the most spectacular element being the magnificent grille in the chancel arch, with an enormous late Gothic crucifix on the rood beam. But even more beautiful is the organ, built in 1669–1672 by Michael Beringel from Szczecin. The decorative organ loft originates from the workshop of Martin Edleber. In the vicinity of the cathedral, there are many beautiful half-timbered houses – this type of architecture has recently been coming back into vogue.

Wolin, across the bay, is Poland's largest island, with a picturesque morainic landscape enhanced by lakes, forests and cliffs. The island was once inhabited by a West Slavonic tribe known as the Volinians, who competed on equal terms with the Vikings in this region of the Baltic. Wolin's attractions include the beach at Międzyzdroje, the seaport at Świnoujście, and the magnificent cliffs, extending over an 11-kilometre stretch of coast and reaching a height of 115 metres. This unique environment is protected by the Wolin National Park. Vegetation on the island is dominated by beech, pine, honeysuckle and ivy. There are six strict reserves on Wolin, the natural habitat of the endangered white-tailed eagle.

1. The cathedral at Kamień Pomorski.
2. The cathedral organ.
3. Old half-timbered houses.

➡ Międzyzdroje – a 19th cent. seaside resort and spa; Świnoujście – popular holiday destination, Poland's largest fishing port, 19th-cent. spa park.

SZCZECIN

Szczecin is a strange town. Historically, it belonged to Poland for a brief period only, and yet when this link was severed, the town declined. Its beginnings go back to a 9th-century Slavonic settlement (surrounded with a 12-metre high timber-laced rampart) guarding a ford across the Odra. It soon evolved into a centre of craftsmanship and trade – a kind of merchant republic which maintained contacts with places as far away as Byzantium. From the 12th century, Szczecin was the outlet through which crops from Wielkopolska were exported to Western Europe, and thus became one of the most important Pomeranian towns. Linked with the Hanseatic League from the 13th century onwards, it enjoyed privileges conferred by Polish and Danish kings. The power of the local Slavonic dukes considerably increased during that period. In 1630, Szczecin was captured by the Swedes, who cut off its traditional commercial links, bringing about the town's rapid decline. In 1713, it became incorporated into Prussia. Sixteen years later, Szczecin was the scene of an event which had the direst consequences for Poland. At the time, however, no one took heed of the birth of Princess Sophie Auguste Fredericka von Anhalt-Zerbst, who many years later would inspire fear and admiration in equal measure under the name of the Czarina Catherine II.

Under Prussian rule, Szczecin began to prosper, reaching an apogee at the turn of the 19th century, by which time it had become one of the most important Baltic ports. The town underwent at that time large-scale modernisation, including the construction of monumental, historicist buildings along today's Wały Chrobrego (Chrobry Embankments). The historical monuments preserved in Szczecin include St. James's parish church from the 14th century, the Gothic Church of SS. Peter and Paul from the 15th century, the Franciscan Church from the 13th-16th centuries, and the Castle of the Pomeranian Dukes from the Piast dynasty, with a burial chapel of the land's former rulers. What is left of the city fortifications are the 18th-century Harbour Gate and the Prussian Homage Gate, as well as the Seven Cloak Tower.

1. The Pomeranian Dukes' Castle.
2. The Bay of Szczecin.

➡ Kolbacz – 12th-cent. Cistercian abbey founded by monks from Denmark, 12th-cent. Conversi House and Abbot's House; Chojna – fragments of the city walls with two preserved gates and three towers.

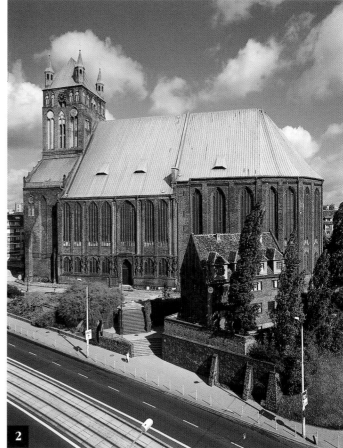

1. *Szczecin Town Hall (13th–15th cent.).*
2. *St. James's Cathedral.*
3. *Corbel decorations in the Church of SS. Peter and Paul (15th cent.).*

➡ Goleniów Forest, Bukowa Forest, Wkrzańska Forest – woodland areas surrounding Szczecin, some of them overlapping the town.

STARGARD SZCZECIŃSKI

Stargard Szczeciński was once an important point at the intersection of trade routes, and the settlement situated there had an important administrative function. In the 12th and 13th centuries, it formed the centre of a local territorial community and then became a castellany. Over the centuries, the town often contended with Szczecin for economic supremacy over Western Pomerania. In 1253, Stargard received from Duke Barnim I a municipal charter based on Magdeburg Law, replaced in 1292 with Lübeck Law. The extant monuments from that period include the 13th-century Gothic parish church, the 15th-century late Gothic parish church, and the medieval Organist's House. Stargard's most magnificent building, the 13th-century parish church, was erected in stages. Its chancel was built in 1380–1400, to a design by the greatest Pomeranian architect of the time, Heinrich Brunsberg. The structure is rich in architectural detail – quoins, traceries and rosettes. As many as 650 types of glazed brick elements of various shapes were used in the decoration. The 15th-century St. John Church, in turn, boasts the highest tower in Western Pomerania – 99 metres. The 13th-century city walls with towers and gates, the late Gothic arsenal and the 16th century fortifications with bastions are relics of a time when Stargard was the mightiest stronghold of Western Pomerania, enjoying special protection as a regional capital. Also worth noting are the Gothic-Renaissance town hall from the 16th century and two 17th-century Baroque buildings: the guard house and municipal weighing house.

The core of Stargard was the Lower Town, situated on an island on the Ina river. The Upper Town was built later. Among the monuments reconstructed after wartime destruction is the town hall, with an extremely elaborate, late Gothic gable. It was built in the 13th century, but owes its final form to a remodelling after a fire of 1540. Near the Rampart Gate is a rare instance of a 2.5-metre penitential stone cross dating from 1542. On the outskirts of town, there is an interesting morainic landscape reserve.

1. St. Mary's Church in Stargard Szczeciński.
2. Inside the nave of St. Mary's.
3. Gothic residential house in Stargard.

➤ Brzesko – stalactite-like decoration of the church ceiling (17th cent.); Drawno National Park – 12 strict reserves for the protection of water sources and lakes, forests, flora, fauna and peat bogs.